# GOLDSTEIN'S GREATEST HITS

## A Book Mostly About Rock 'n' Roll

BY

RICHARD GOLDSTEIN

PRENTICE-HALL, INC. • ENGLEWOOD CLIFFS, N.J.

We gratefully acknowledge permission to print selections
and articles which first appeared in the following: *Eye
Magazine;* © 1968 by the Hearst Corporation. *New
York Magazine;* © 1966, 1967, 1968 by New York
Magazine Co. *The New York Times;* © 1967, 1969 by
The New York Times Company; reprinted by permission.
*The Village Voice;* © 1966, 1967, 1968 by *The Village
Voice. West Magazine,* the Los Angeles *Times.*

*This is dedicated
to the one I love.*

"WHAT D'YA DIG MOST ABOUT
DONOVAN?" I ONCE ASKED A GIRL
WITH CHEEKS LIKE CHEWING GUM,
AND SHE THREW BACK HER HAIR
AND GIGGLED: "I LIKE HIS RIG."

Except for "Liner Notes," all the pieces in this book were written between 1966 and 1968. I look upon them as snapshots, designed to capture a specific image while it was still visible. These aren't analytical essays about emotions reflected upon in tranquility, but immediate impressions recorded hot off the head. I don't intend this book to serve as the definitive history of rock, nor do I want to offer an inclusive explanation for its appeal. My goal is to convey the vitality of pop, not as it happened, but as I discovered it—between margins, between deadlines, between awe and envy.

To preserve something of that immediacy, I have chosen to include phrases and sentiments which may seem awkward now, in the light of overuse. Nothing has less chic than year-old slang. Though I have done some editing on these pieces (and in a few cases, have combined similar columns on the same subject) parts of this book will seem dated: that's as it should be. I mean *Goldstein's Greatest Hits* to be a scrapbook, and you don't edit nostalgia for timeliness.

If there is any development in tone or viewpoint here, it is from the wonder in my early columns to the reserve which came later, when being a "critic" had already become a profession and a task. That feeling of obligation, coupled with what I sensed as a loss of vitality on the scene, was the reason why, early in 1969, I decided to curtail my writing on rock and explore other, less trammeled areas of pop culture.

Re-reading these essays with that choice in mind, I feel like I'm looking at a picture of myself as a virgin—all pink and pudgy and ready to be captivated, and I was. I don't think I'll ever feel blasé about the polar-bear genius who destroyed his music because he thought it would start fires. Or the spade goddess who farted in the middle of an interview. Or the record company executive who offered hashish from a bronze butterfly. I've seen a lot of people with their heads gloriously shattered. I learned to take notes while stoned.

v

I learned to read press releases without opening the envelopes. I learned to put myself in corners and fade into the entourage. Most important, I learned that I could never function as a superstar-by-proxy. Today, I have to admit, most of my close friends are other writers.

I want to thank Dan Wolf, editor of the *Village Voice,* who first let me run free in his pages, and Clay Felker, editor of *New York Magazine,* who taught me about the difference between rapping and writing. I consider these men close friends, and it shakes me up a little to think that they're both over thirty.

# CONTENTS

# LINER NOTES

Here's how I write
in a straight-back chair
sweatsocks and underwear
hair pulled tight behind the ears
squeezing, twitching, sucking
the ends of my moustache.
Writing is heavy shit
solid like lead or loose like mud.
Is it a boy or a girl, doctor?
I dunno, but it's got flecks of corn in it.


Khaki freak
too much by eighty pounds.
Wore that sweater
till it up and tattered.
Went fishing in the ruins
of Catholic mystery.
I was Jesus
they were Jews
crucifixion on the concourse.
We picked a fight
with three greasers

ix

then hobbled back to shul
and watched from the balcony
those stained-glass faces
the weighted dominos
all bobbing holyholy.
We giggled touched each other
and wiped the pews
with snot.


Home was where
in the winter
they had to give you heat.
Rhododendron agony
all kinds cheeses
in the martyr's brain.
What was it like to be crazy there?
Like eating snow
first cold then warm.
You couldn't scream
Your balls collided nightly
You had to jerk off in the bathroom.


Ran away at three
with just a bowtie on.
Rubbed firefly glow
on my belt to make me grow.
Got laid one summer
how I blew that one
all sweat inside
and fingers everywhere.
Do we do it here?


Remember when
we slept without forgiving
and woke up tangled
in each other's hairs?

Alma mater
army in tweed
the world before me
like an oreo.
I learned to march
and suave as seltzer
sang my centaur's song:

    Richard Goldstein
    reporter for the Kokomo *Morning Times*
    died today at his desk.
    He was 21-years-old.
    His mother dressed him funny.
    Mr. Goldstein joined the *Times*
    after 20 years as a free agent
    and nine months as a creampuff.
    He had also worked as a fetish.
    A reporter for the *Times*
    who refused to be offset
    said Mr. Goldstein died of overkill
    but inflamed sources indicate
    he suffered cuts, bruises, and lacerations
    following an encounter
    with his ego.
    thirty

Beware death by water.
Mommy bathed him naked Mondays
and every Friday clipped his nails
dancing around him in procession
the cop jabbed once
then up his arms his eyes and belly heart
till the kid fell bleeding spit
heels into nipples
the rush of pure assault
his eyes shot up and outasight.
This really happened.

I saw the best minds of my generation
clubbed and coddled
bagged and bottled
meat raw muscle
in the hubcap of my heart
kookie kookie
lend me your chrome.
I'm with you in rock land
but I don't need your ritual
of holy agony.
With rock to seethe the savage beast
to summon Stones against Goliath
to stop
to stun
to realize I am myself
of a kind
of a place
of a power.
POWPOWPOW.

# I
# GEAR

# ● GEAR

Too early to get up, especially on Saturday. The sun peeks over his windowsill. Isolated footsteps from the street. Guys who have to work on Saturday. Boy! That's what they'll call you all your life if you don't stay in school. Forty-five definitions, two chapters in *Silas Marner,* and three chem labs. On Sunday night, he will sit in his room with the radio on, bobbing back and forth on his bed, opening the window wide and then closing it, taking a break to eat, to comb his hair, to dance, to hear the Stones—anything. Finally, cursing wildly and making ugly faces at himself in the mirror, he will throw *Silas Marner* under the bed and spend an hour watching his tortoise eat lettuce.

In the bathroom he breaks three screaming pimples. With a toothpick he removes four specks of food from his braces, skirting barbed wires and week-old rubber bands. Brooklyn Bridge, railroad tracks, they called him. Metal mouth. They said he smiled like someone was forcing him to. Bent fingers with filthy nails. Caved-in chest with eight dangling hairs. A face that looks like the end of a watermelon, and curly hair—not like the Stones, not at all like Brian Jones—but muddy curls running down his forehead and over his ears. A bump. Smashed by a bat thrown wildly. When he was eight. Hunchback Quasimodo—Igor—Rodan on his head. A bump. Nobody hip has a bump or braces. Or hair like a fucking Frankenstein movie. He licks his braces clean and practices smiling.

3

Hair straight and heavy. Nose full. Lips bulging like boiling frankfurters. Hung. Bell bottoms and boss black boots. He practices his Brian Jones expressions. Fist held close to the jaw. Ready to spring, ready to spit. Evil. His upper brace catches on a lip.

He walks past his parents' room, where his mother sleeps in a gauzy hairnet, the covers pulled over her chin, her baby feet swathed in yellow calluses. Her hand reaches over to the night table where her eyedrops and glasses lie. He mutters silently at her. The night before there had been a fight—the usual fight, with Mommy shouting "I'll give you money! Sure, you rotten kid! I'll give you clothing so you can throw it all over the floor—that's blood money in those pants of yours!" And him answering the usual "geh-awf-mah-bak" and her: "Don't you yell at me, don't you—did you hear that (to no one). Did you hear how that kid . . . ?" and him slamming the door—the gray barrier—and above the muffled ". . . disrespects his mother . . . He treats me like dirt under his feet! . . . and he wants me to buy him . . . he'll spit on my grave". . . and finally dad's groaning shuffle and a murmured "Ronnie, you better shut your mouth to your mother," and him whispering silently, the climactic, the utter: "Fucking bitch. Cunt. Cunt."

Now she smiles. So do crocodiles. He loves her. He doesn't know why he cursed, except that she hates it. It was easy to make her cry and though he shivers at the thought of her lying across the bed sobbing into a pillow, her housedress pulled slightly over a varicose thigh, he has to admit doing it was easy.

On the table he sees the pants she bought him yesterday. Her money lining his pocket, he had taken the bus to Fordham Road and in Alexander's he had cased out the Mod rack. Hands shaking, dying for a cigarette, he found the pants—a size small but still a fit. He bought them, carried them home clutched in his armpit, and deposited them before her during prime "Star Trek" TV time.

"Get away. I can't see. Whatsamaddah, your father a glazier or something?" And when he unveiled the pants and asked for the usual cuff-making ritual (when he would stand on the ladder and she, holding a barrage of pins in her mouth, would run the tailor's chalk along his shoe line and make him drag out the old black sewing machine), the fight began—and ended within the hour. The pants, hemmed during "The Merv Griffin Show" as the last

labor of the night, now lay exposed and sunlit on the table. $8.95 pants.

They shimmer. The houndstooth design glows against the formica. Brown and green squares are suddenly visible within the gray design. He brushes the fabric carefully so the wool bristles. He tries them on, zipping up the two-inch fly, thinking at first that he has broken the zipper until he realizes that hip-huggers have no fly to speak of. They buckle tightly around his hips, hug his thighs, and flare suddenly at his knees. He races to the mirror and grins.

His hips are suddenly tight and muscular. His waist is sleek and his ass round and bulging. Most important, the pants make him look hung. Like the kids in the park. The odor of stale cigarettes over their clothing, medallions dangling out of their shirts. Their belt buckles ajar. They are hip. They say "Check out that bike." Get bent on Gypsy. Write the numbers of cruising police cars all over the walls. ROT, they call themselves. Reign of Terror. In the park they buzz out on glue, filling paper bags and breathing deeply, then sitting on the grass slopes, watching the cars. Giggling. Grooving. High.

Sometimes they let him keep the models that come with the glue. Or he grubs around their spot until, among the torn bags and oozing tubes, he finds a Messerschmitt or Convair spread across the grass ruins as though it had crashed there.

He unzips his pants and lets them hang on the door where he can watch them from the living room. He takes a box of Oreos from the kitchen, stacking the cookies in loose columns on the rug. He pours a cup of milk and turns on the TV. Farmer Gray runs nervously up and down the screen while a pig squats at ease by his side. His pants are filled with hornets. He runs in a cloud of dust toward a pond which appears and disappears teasingly, leaving Farmer Gray grubbing in the sand. Outasight!

He fills his mouth with three Oreos and wraps his feet around the screen so he can watch Farmer Gray between his legs. Baby habit. Eating cookies on the floor and watching cartoons on Saturday morning. Like thumbsucking. They teased him about it until he threw imaginary furniture into their faces. A soft bulge on his left thumb from years of sucking—cost them a fortune in braces. Always busting his hump.

He kills the TV picture and puts the radio on softly, because he

doesn't want to wake Daddy who is asleep on his cot in the middle of the living room, bunched up around the blanket, his face creased in a dream, hands gripping his stomach in mock tension. Daddy snores in soft growls.

He brushes a flock of Oreo crumbs under the TV and rubs a milk stain into the rug. Thrown out of your own bed for snoring. You feel cheap, like Little Bo Peep; beep beep beep beep.

There is nothing to stop him from going downstairs. The guys are out already, slung over cars and around lampposts. The girls are trickling out of the project. It's cloudy, but until it actually rains he knows they will be around the lamppost, spitting out into the street, horsing around, grubbing for hooks, singing. He finishes four more cookies and stuffs half an apple onto his chocolate-lined tongue.

Marie Giovanni put him down bad for his braces. When she laughs her tits shake. Her face is pink; her hair rises in a billowing bouffant. In the hallway, she let Tony get his fingers wet. Yesterday she cut on him; called him metal mouth.

He flicks the radio off, grabs the pants from the hanger, and slides into them. He digs out a brown turtleneck from under a rubble of twisted clothing (they dress him like a ragpicker) and shines his boots with spit. They are chipping and the heels are worn on one side, but they make him look an inch taller, so he wears them whenever he can.

He combs his hair in the mirror. Back on the sides, over the ears, so the curl doesn't show. Over the eyes in the front to cover up his bump. Straight down the back of his neck, so it rests on his collar. He checks his bald spot for progress and counts the hairs that come out in his brush. In two years he knows he will be bald in front and his bump will look like a boulder on his forehead.

He sits on his bed and turns the radio on. From under the phonograph he lifts a worn fan magazine—Pop in bright fuchsia lettering—with Zal Yanovsky hunched over one P, Paul McCartney contorted over the other, and Nancy Sinatra touching her toes around the O. He turns to the spread on the Stones and flips the pages until he sees The Picture. Mick Jagger and Marianne Faithfull. Mick scowling, waving his fingers in the air. Marianne watching the camera. Marianne, waiting for the photographer to shoot.

Marianne. Marianne, eyes fading brown circles, lips slightly parted in flashbulb surprise, miniskirt spread apart, tits like two perfect cones under her sweater. He had to stop looking at Marianne Faithfull a week ago.

He turns the page and glances at the shots of Brian Jones and then his eyes open wide because a picture in the corner shows Brian in Ronnie's pants. The same check. The same rise and flare. Brian leaning against a wall, his hands on the top of his magic hip-huggers. Wick-ked!

He flips the magazine away and stands in a curved profile against the mirror. He watches the pants move as he does. From a nearby flowerpot he gathers a fingerful of dirt and rubs it over his upper lip. He checks hair, nose, braces, nails, and pants. He likes the pants. They make him look hung. He reaches into his top drawer and pulls out a white handkerchief. He opens his fly and inserts the rolled cloth, patting it in place, and closing the zipper over it. He looks boss. Unfuckinbelievable.

In the elevator Ronnie takes a cigarette from his three-day-old pack and keeps it unlit in his mouth. Marie Giovanni will look at his pants and giggle. Tony will bellow "Check out them pants," and everyone will groove on them. In the afternoon, they will take him down to the park and turn him on, and he will feel the buzz they are always talking about and the cars will speed by like sparks.

Brian Jones thoughts in his head. Tuff thoughts. He will slouch low over the car and smoke with his thumb over the cigarette— the hip way. And when he comes back upstairs they will finally get off his back. Even on Fordham Road, where the Irish kids crack up when he walks by, even in chemistry and gym, they will know who he is and nod a soft "hey" when he comes by. He'll get laid.

Because clothing IS important. Especially if you've got braces and bony fingers and a bump the size of a goddam coconut on your head.

And especially if you're fourteen. Because—ask anyone. Fourteen is shit.

—THE VILLAGE VOICE, 1966

# THE SOUL SOUND FROM SHEEPSHEAD BAY

They started with a twinkle in their eyes and leatherette on their hips. Out there on the stage of the Brooklyn Fox, with Murray the K, a thousand kids, and all that dripping rococo.

They started in clinging blue jeans and long, limp hair. Knee-high boots. Wailing. The three of them swaying while a guy circles the stage on a real motorcycle, revving the motor. Chrome and lipstick gleaming in the spotlight.

The girl in the center—the one they call Mary Weiss—puts the mike down her throat and (*OHWOW*) sobs with soul, and her eyes are open wide and blue.

> My folks were always putting him down
> They said he comes from the wrong side of town
> They told me he was bad
> But I knew he was sad
> That's why I fell for
> The leader of the pack.*

So much for the early Shangri-Las. This is the Aquarian age (at least it was last time I consulted my guru). Now the leather and scruffy jeans have been replaced by bell-bottom slacks, shaggy bangs, and a pair of 98-cent Weegie glasses.

\* Copyright by Trio Music Co., Inc., Tender Tunes Music Co., Inc., and Elmwin Music, Inc.

8

The faces, too, are different. A little less hairspray in those smiles. A little looseness around those pouting lips. Well, the Shangri-Las may have changed their image, but their music remains intact. The Soul Sound from Sheepshead Bay has survived the enlightenment.

They are Maryann, Betty, and Mary. Two sisters and a friend from the same block in Cambria Heights, Queens. But you can find kids like them under the el in Rockaway, under the lamppost on Broadway. On street corners anywhere and everywhere in New York. They belong to summer nights spent in sidewalk pizzerias, to sweltering boredom and cold street wants. Their look and sound are the city. And if soul means evoking super-reality, the Shangri-Las have it, blue eyes, glottal stops, and all.

"We try to stay real close to our audience," says Mary. "Most kids have a hangup with their parents, and a lot of girls want to be the center of attention the way the girl in 'Leader of the Pack' is. These are the kids who listen to us."

Though the girls have played colleges and adult clubs ("It's a different scene with adults. They love our songs about jilted parents"), their steady public is composed of thirteen-to-seventeen-year-old girls. Says Mary: "They may buy the Supremes, but they listen to us. Because the Supremes come on very feminine and chic, but we come on like the average girl, who just isn't slinky and sexy. We couldn't do all those oozy 'baby, babys,' but the Supremes couldn't get away with 'Leader of the Pack.'"

There is something eternal about the Shangri-Las, something mythic. Talk about the suffering teenager. Their heroines are the victims of high parental tragedy. But they remain loyal and passionate. They persevere. The kids in these songs have never heard of the Cool Generation. They are actively, hopelessly involved. Crying is one sign of sincerity in a Shangri-La song; it never implies cowardice or loss of cool. The too-young lovers in "Give Us Your Blessing" run away from their righteous parents with tears in their eyes, only to die in an auto crash. The hero of "Leader of the Pack" goes to his death misty-eyed and martyred.

> He sorta smiled and kissed me goodbye
> But the tears were beginning to show
> As he drove away on that rainy night

> I begged him to go slow
> But whether he heard I'll never know . . .
>
> CHORUS: Look out! Look out! Look out! *
>
> (sound of screeching tires, shattered glass,
> mashed metal, and burning leather boots.)

The anti-hero in motorcycle drag is a recurrent figure in Shangri-La songs. He moves through life as a victim, downtrodden and reeking of delinquency. What he needs, obviously, is a little love. So, in "Give Him a Great Big Kiss," his best girl exults: "When I say I'm in love, you'd best believe I'm in love, L-U-V." The dialogue between narrator and chorus which follows should be read as tin pan alley verité.

> What kuluh are his eyes?
> I dunno, he's always wearing shades.
> Yeah? Well, I heah he's bad
> Mmmm? He's good-bad, but he's not evil.

In "Out in the Streets," our anti-hero:

> Grew up on the sidewalks
> Street lights shinin' above
> He grew up with no one to love.

But then he is saved, only to suffer the agonies of respectability (i.e.—clean fingernails):

> He don't comb his hair
> Like he did before
> He don't wear those dirty old black boots no more
> He used to act bad
> Used to—but he quit it
> It makes me so sad
> 'Cause I know that he did it
> For me. . . .†

Rebellious passion is the Shangri-Las' major theme, and the conflict between that passion and filial obligation is the grist of

* *Ibid.*
† Copyright by Trio Music Co., Inc.

their melodrama. "I Can Never Go Home Anymore," their master-piece (you knew that word would come up in this article), deals with the separation from Mother on the most ruthless adolescent terms. It is precipitated by sexuality, and followed by remorse. Its ambience is Yiddish-universal; its intensity is both high tragedy and low camp.

The song opens with a spoken threat. "I'm gonna hide if she don't leave me alone." But the chorus (dramatically Greek but emotionally Jewish) warns: "Don't! 'Cause you can never go home anymore."

> You wake up every morning
> Go to school every day
> Spend your nights on the corner
> Just passin' time away. . . .
> And then a miracle,
> A boy.

Mother says she's too young, and that she feels not love but "girlish pride." The narrator packs her bag(s) and moves on. But not before she recalls—in full stereo if you've got the album—a Yiddish lullaby her mother used to sing. Even this recollection is interrupted, however, by a piercing shriek which puts Sophocles on Second Avenue: M-A-M-A! The tempo quickens. Drums pound like indigestion. A chorus intones—in Oedipal terror—"You can never go home anymore!" while the speaker screams again "M-A-M-A!" A crescendo of violins brings us back to the dominant melody and the moral:

> Don't do to your mom
> What I did to mine
> She grew so lonely in the end
> The angels picked her for a friend
> And I can never—go home—anymore.*

"Of course it's a long way up, and you never think you'll get there," Mary recalls. "The first time you're onstage with all that equipment backing you up, it's a weird feeling. But then you kind of become part of the show. That's the way it was with us. After a

* Copyright by Trio Music Co., Inc.

while, we weren't wearing pants and sweaters because they were comfortable, but as a uniform. We stopped being teenagers. I think we kind of lost our sight.

"That's how it happens to everyone, I think. Dylan . . . The Beatles . . . everyone. Things that thrill you change. And suddenly, you stop being a kid from Queens and what you become is . . . well, a professional teenager."

Betty Weiss, her sister Mary, and her friend Maryann Ganser are in pop music because rock 'n' roll is to middle-class teenagers what boxing was to the poor: a chance to make it. They were discovered three and a half years ago, during a hop at Saint Michael's Catholic School, in the Bay Ridge section of Brooklyn. Shadow Morton, a fledgling record producer, happened to be scouting that evening. And since producers are key men in pop music (they can turn an image into a singing group, an idea into a product, a recording into a hit)—the Shangri-Las said sure, okay.

It's been a long ride from Cambria Heights. Mary, slouched in an easy chair and sipping a malted, recalls the group's first TV appearance: "It was on the Clarke Race Show in Pittsburgh. We didn't know anything about TV. We wore skirts and white shell blouses. We didn't have any make-up on. So we shone like a bunch of headlights. Boy, did we come on amateur. The audience held its breath for us. Then afterward, this fourteen-year-old kid came up and said, 'Don't worry, you'll make it.' "

Today, TV doesn't frighten Mary Weiss. When she fluffs a line, she reads over it. She moves slowly and smoothly on camera. And she prefers powder blue to glaring white.

"Hey, Mary, you don't look like you do on TV."

"Whatdyamean?"

"You're sultrier on TV."

"Yeah? What d'z sulchry mean?"

"Like, sexy."

"Y'mean I'm not sexy now? He says I'm not sexy."

"No. I mean, like when the kid in the third row sees you and he kind of says 'Oh Wow' at you—how does that feel?"

A long pause at the other end of that question. Finally she answers, into the depths of her malted: "Uh—the Village Voice— that's near Trude Heller's club, right?"

You could call that shyness, reticence, or the good manners not to call someone a shmuck. You can't tell with Mary. Her sister, Betty, is a lot easier to figure out. She opens her blue eyes wide, and just lets it out. "Dylan's got a lot of guts. I think he's like us, in a lot of ways. I mean, what he's saying. What his stuff means. I guess its psychedelic . . . trip music, and all. But it's more than that. I mean, it's good to have that kind of stuff out in the open. Kids know a lot more today; they're hipper. Yeah, I think Dylan is a genius. He's probably a genius."

For her part, Maryann is terse, volatile, opinionated: "They say our stuff is corny, well a lot of people eat corn. Besides, if that were true, then we wouldn't sell. Which we do. Our lines are realistic and frank. Take our latest single. The girl who's talking in it has had one tragic affair, right, and she is obviously hung up on it. Well, we don't put her down for it."

"Past, Present, and Future," the record under discussion, is well within the Shangri-La syndrome. Its narrator looks in retrospect upon the remnants of her affair. "Was I ever in love? I called it love." The Moonlight Sonata fills the background. "There were moments when . . . well, there were moments when."

And then the present:

> Go out with you? Why not?
> Take a walk along the beach tonight? I'd love to.
> But don't try to touch me. . . .
> 'Cause that will never happen again.*

Strains of Beethoven—symbolic of weltzschmertz, you dig?—break through the rolling surf. The future looks bleak indeed. But ennui is a shaggy dog story in a Shangri-La song. Every mood must have a silver lining. It says much for their honesty, and for their authenticity, that "Past, Present, and Future" ends on a note of deflated realism. "At the moment, it doesn't look good," sighs the narrator. "At the moment it'll never happen again."

Some day, of course, they are going to erect a statue of the Shangri-Las, and then those three girls will be immortalized. Picture it: Mary and Betty sitting on a beach towel (you can barely

* Copyright by Trio Music Co., Inc.

make it out, but the towel says "Kiss Me I'm Irish"), and Maryann standing tall, with her hands outstretched like the Christ of the Andes, around them, swarms of teenagers, a transistorized cacophony, and Shadow Morton as a very old man, giving an interview to the press.

"How did they dance, Shadow?"

"Kuh-lose. Ferry, ferry klose."

—THE VILLAGE VOICE, 1966

# ● A QUIET EVENING AT THE BALLOON FARM

Mixed media. Lots of light. Noise enough to make your ears sing back. Blows the mind.

Okay; a psychedelic discotheque. But what's with this balloon farm thing?

Bob Dylan named it. You're supposed to figure out what it means to you.

Inside, there's this couple. Dancing. The girl, in a paisley shift and tree-bark stockings, seems to be moving to some internal rhythm. Her partner is bathed in light: electric blue. He swings low, encircling her waist without touching. His tongue darts snake-like toward her hips, retreating as she grinds forward. The girl takes off her glasses and hands them to her partner. She swoops as the walls play a strobe-lit threnody. Wow—you don't see that stuff on "Hullabaloo."

The dance is called "The Gobble." It started on the Lower East Side, with the Fugs. Now, they're grinding out that kind of hip ritual in Forest Hills (where a spade is something you garden with). But the Gobble can be done anywhere. Which is fortunate, because the Balloon Farm is not your average rock-'n'-ravage joint. The place has atmosphere. Originally called the Dom (which is Polish for "home"), it's a huge, mirrored ballroom where generations of immigrants came to dance, drink, and maybe find a little affection. The men's rooms still retain that compelling stench of wine and sausage.

15

The dance floor is still scuffed from the pounding of a million stomping polkas. Even though the hippies have made St. Mark's Place their drag, the old gestalt lingers on, haunting the Balloon Farm with the irony of a Straight tradition.

Which brings us to Andy Warhol. This is Andy's club so it shows his movies. On one screen, a lady who is possibly a man munches away on a ripe banana. ("I don't give a damn; either way, it's suggestive," says a timid soul to my right.) On another screen, someone is eating peanuts, cracking the shells, gnawing the insides, spitting out the husks. And on the center screen, they have tied someone to a chair and are putting cigarettes out in his nose, winding belts around his neck, and fitting a tight leather mask over his face. Just like in the movies!

That's called "Vinyl." Its creator (call him "A-a-ah-ndy," and smile a lot when you say that) is sitting quietly in the balcony. He is working the projector, pensive and subdued in his black-chino-polo-shirt-leather-jacket-uniform. Close-up, his face is leathery as well. Mirror sunglasses make his eyes totally inaccessible. His hair is straight, bright silver.

"Hi," he says.

"Who's the peanut man?" you ask, to return the greeting.

"Henry."

"Uh-huh."

"Geldzahler."

"Isn't he with the Jordanaires," you long to ask, but you content yourself with a soft, knowing, "Beautiful.")

He turns back to the projector, his fingers busily shuffling tins of film. Lights crackle like horsewhips around him. ("When it looks like they're enjoying it, he makes it all go faster," someone near me offers.) Onstage, Gerard Malanga grabs a roll of phosphorescent tape and wraps it around his partner and himself. Handed a whip, he snaps it in time to the strobes. As a finale, he smothers his body in yellow paint and grabs a purple spotlight, which makes him glow and deepens the shadow around his eyes and teeth. Speed zone. He untangles two blinking strobe lights and swings them around his hips, sending violent, stabbing rays into the audience. ("At least he didn't piss on us," I heard a teeniebopper whisper; her friend grumbled back, "they said he would, too.")

Definitely light. For the next ten minutes, electricity becomes a weapon of frontal assault. Bulbs blink patterns onto the ceiling and the mirrored walls. Colored sparks twinkle ominously and those two portable strobes make your entire line of vision sway. It's all very much like sitting stoned in the middle of a tinseled Christmas tree.

"Okay," says the girl in the tree-bark stockings. "It's a little confusing at first, I'll admit. My shrink could probably give out calling cards at the exit. But . . . see . . . it's like one of those connect the dots pictures, where everything is jumbled until you take a pencil and put it all together. Then it becomes a picture—it makes sense."

Which brings us to the Velvet Underground, not a first class car on the London transit system, but Andy's rock group. Sometimes they sing, sometimes they just stroke their instruments into a single, hour-long jam. Their sound is a savage series of atonal thrusts and electronic feedback. Their lyrics combine sado-masochistic frenzy with free-association imagery. The whole thing seems to be the product of a secret marriage between Bob Dylan and the Marquis De Sade. It takes a lot to laugh; it takes a train to cry.

Andy says he is through with phosphorescent flowers and cryptic soupcans. Now it's rock. He may finally conquer the world through its soft, teenage underbelly.

"It's ugly," he admits. "It's a very ugly effect when you put it all together. But it's beautiful. You know, you just look at the whole thing—the Velvets playing and Gerard dancing and all the film and light, and it's a beautiful thing. Very Vinyl. Beautiful."

"Yeah, beautiful. There are beautiful sounds in rock. Very lazy, dreamlike noises. You can forget about the lyrics in most songs. Just dig the noise, and you've got our sound. We're putting everything together—lights and film and music—and we're reducing it to its lowest common denominator. We're musical primitives."

That's John Cale, composer, guitarist, and resident Welshman for the Velvet Underground. He plays a mean, slashing viola. And piano, when he has to. He and Lou Reed once shared a three-room flat on Ludlow Street and a group called the Primitives. Their place was cold (broken crates in a wood-burning fireplace looked very chic but also kept the blood circulating). The group was cold too, bassman Sterling Morrison recalls: "Sometimes we'd do more jumping around in a night than the goddam waitresses. Before Andy

saw us at the Cafe Bizarre (which isn't exactly the Copa of MacDougal Street) we were busting our balls in work. Up to here. And you can't do anything creative when you're struggling to keep the basic stuff coming. Now it seems we have time to catch our breath. We have more direction—that's where Andy comes in. We eat better, we work less, and we've found a new medium for our music. It's one thing to hustle around for odd jobs. But now we're not just another band; we're an act. See—when a band becomes an act, you get billing. You get days off. You don't just work nights—you're, like, Engaged."

Nightly at the Balloon Farm the Velvets demonstrate what distinguishes an act from a band. They are special. They even have a chanteuse—Nico, who is half goddess, half icicle. If you say bad things about her singing, she doesn't talk to you. If you say nice things, she doesn't talk to you either. If you say that she sounds like a bellowing moose, she might smile if she digs the sound of that in French. Onstage, she is somewhat less communicative. But she sings in perfect mellow ovals. It sounds something like a cello getting up in the morning. All traces of melody depart early in her solo. The music courses into staccato beats, then slows into syrupy feedback. All this goes on until everyone is satisfied that the point has gotten across.

Oh yeah; the point! John Cale sits dreamily eyeing a Coke, pushes his hair back from his face to expose a bony nose, and observes: "You can't pin it down." (Granted.) "It's a conglomeration of the senses. What we try to get here is a sense of total involvement." (You mean acid, scoobie-doobie-doo?)

"Coming here on a trip is bound to make a tremendous difference. But we're here to stimulate a different kind of intoxication. The sounds, the visual stuff—all this bombarding of the senses—it can be very heady in itself, if you're geared to it."

John Cale is a classicist. His first composition was "written on a rather large piece of plywood." He studied viola and piano at the London Conservatory of Music and came to the United States as a Leonard Bernstein fellow. His sponsor was Aaron Copland. "We didn't get on very well," John says. "Copland said I couldn't play my work at Tanglewood. It was too destructive, he said. He didn't want his piano wrecked."

Cale pursued his vision with John Cage. On the viola, he would play a single note for as long as two hours. Then he met Lou Reed, and the sound that John calls "controlled distortion" was born.

The Velvets, with Nico and Andy and all that light, began to construct a scene around the title "Exploding Plastic Inevitable." They've done quite a bit of traveling since, and their reviews reflect the ambivalence a quiet evening at the Balloon Farm can produce. Said the *Chicago Daily News:* "The flowers of evil are in full bloom." *Los Angeles* magazine compared the sound to "Berlin in the decadent thirties." Even Cher (of Sonny and Cher) was heard to mutter: "It will replace nothing except suicide."

Dauntless, the troupe returned home. Now they are popping eardrums and brandishing horsewhips on a nightly basis. Their first album sounds a bit restrained (though a long, harrowing cut called "Heroin" isn't exactly calculated to make the radio as a "good-guy sure-shot"). But it's still The Sound. And the group is brimming with innovation.

"We want to try an electronic drum," says John. "It would produce sub-sonic sounds, so you could feel it even when you couldn't hear it. We'd then be able to add it to a piece of music, and it would be like underlining the beat" (in cement).

Onstage, Gerard Malanga motions wildly. They have run out of records, and that means it's time for another set. John puts down his Coke and wraps a black corduroy jacket over his turtleneck. He slides his hair over his face, covering his nose again. Lou tucks his shirt in.

"Young people know where everything is at," he says. "Let 'em sing about going steady on the radio. Let 'em run their hootenannies. But it's in holes like this that the real stuff is being born. The university and the radio kill everything, but around here, it's alive. The kids know that."

The girl in the bark stockings is leaning against the stage, watching them warm up. "You can tell this is going to be a very atonal set," she says. "It's something about the way they handle their instruments when they first come onstage."

"Beautiful," sighs her partner, rolling his larynx and his eyes. With a single humming chord, which seems to hang in the air, the Velvet Underground launches into another set. John squints against

a purple spotlight. Lou shouts against a groaning amplifier. Gerard writhes languidly to one side. Sterling turns his head to sneeze. And Nico stands there, looking haunted. The noise, the lights, the flickering images—all happen. Everybody grooves.

From the balcony, Andy Warhol watches from behind his glasses. "Beautiful," he whispers. Sterling sneezes audibly but it seems to fit. "Beautiful." Gerard hands his partner a bullwhip and the girl in bark begins to sway. "Just beautiful."

—NEW YORK MAGAZINE, 1966

# ● THE DRUIDS OF STONEHENGE

They're the best pop group on the upper West Side.

Carl Hauser, the 18-year-old lead guitarist, has the longest hair (straight brown strands which ovalize his face). This is so that when they whistle at him on Flatbush Avenue, he can call them cretin holdovers from the Vitalis days.

Tom Workman, on bass, is a 19-year-old senior in Columbia's pre-med program. He admits he can't see hanging out his shingle on the Grand Concourse with a hundred thousand pop-star dollars in the bank. But he doesn't know which alternative will pan out: AMA or AGVA.

Steve Tindall, 19, handles percussion, which means he sweats to make his drums heard above a powerhouse of amplified guitars. His suit is tweedy; his boots don't button all the way up his leg; his shapeless Eton cap sits like an onion roll on his head. Steve will make the gray-flannel transformation easiest of all. It shows in his socks.

Bill Tracy, the 18-year-old guitarist, sits quietly to one side, coaxing sound from his electric umbilical cord. A philo major at Columbia, Tracy's face curdles under a mane of orange excelsior hair. Tracy's parents own a building on Riverside Drive, and the group takes periodic possession of the tiny basement as a rehearsal hall.

Dave Budge is a 21-year-old Lit bum at the New School. He does

the singing. In brightly striped hip-huggers and a poor-boy sweater, he stands curled around the mike, his teeth bucking as he spits out note after note. He winds his arms, waves his hands, and points accusingly at the audience. This means Dave Budge has been watching Mick Jagger. When he sings, his face gets red, and his shoulders shudder. Jagger and Budge may move alike, but Jagger's face never gets red anymore.

All together they call themselves the Druids of Stonehenge. Their turf is Tracy's basement—a claustrophobic closet decorated in raw plaster and grease. They set up. It takes 20 minutes to connect the proper wires and tune the appropriate dials. When the whole room emits dull hum, everything is ready. The equipment—gaping black amplifiers, twanging strings, and loose connections—constitutes the group's personal treasure. When a beginning rock musician switches groups, he usually brings his equipment with him. The Druids have thus ransomed their amplifiers from other combos. Dead and buried associations from the short-haired Great-Sting-Ray-Daytona days pop up like so much Hittite History. The Ramrods, The Sidewinders. Six dollars a night at the Cafe Bizarre. A high school hop in 1962. Carl modestly asserts: "I invented rock 'n' roll in the Village 12 years ago."

Together and tuned up—with equipment that does not quite match—the Druids of Stonehenge launch into a set with "It's All Over Now Baby Blue," the Dylan standard. Dave is a blushing James Brown, screeching into the mike. Waves of stinging sound fill the tiny basement, loosening a column of roaches from the ceiling beams. The song does not end; it subsides. The top settles back. But then there is another number—Bo Diddley's "I'm a Man." And another—"Blue Suede Shoes," with pseudo-Presley modulations and background harmonies that a Jordanaire would be proud to call his own.

Tom shakes his head free of vibrations. A rock musician's ears soon becomes whetstone to loud noise. "Playing like this is a complete relaxation from school," says Tom. "It's an absolute purgative."

Informal rehearsals—with a generous encouragement from groupies huddled in a corner—are the fun part. Last year, says Tom, "We did nothing but play frat dances. It's a terrible scene; a

real drag. There's this overwhelming odor of stale beer about a frat house. Nobody's there to listen to your music; they just wanna do the Boston Monkey. They spill beer all over us. They bellow into our mike . . . foamies . . . greasers . . ."

The others join in: Pighead-crewcuts. Jocks. Biting the hand that feeds you a crumb is always a groove. But no university group can exist without a stipend from the fraternities. The Druids and a local group called the Walkers (Carl modestly calls them "our protege") are the big draws at Columbia this year. The Druids say they hate the frat-circuit. But it pays up to $165 a dance, and they love the money.

Words like greaser and foamy pockmark Druid-patter. The student put-down is a happening in itself. It begins in the cerebellum, moves to the recesses of the throat and comes whizzing forth between clenched teeth. In the ultimate reaction, everyone snickers and turns away from the target; he is left to cry in his West End beer.

Carl arches his back, like a rooster about to spit on Farmer Brown, then lets loose a torrent of cool abuse. He is down on most groups in the business, as well as truck drivers, Barnard girls, and folk singers. But he's up this month on psychedelic living. He reveals, "I want to be a plumb in the midst of nature . . . you can quote that line . . . it's from Walt Whitman."

It hasn't been long since the Druids made the jump from grease to acid rock. They revel in the change. Dave says: "Real trip songs are hard to write. Psychedelic music means improvisations, but worrying about what everyone else is playing at the same time. In good acid rock, you don't just get a mess of noise. Every new sound is a surprise, but it's all intricately interwoven and spontaneous. Like a tapestry coming out of the clouds, it's free-form melody."

The Druids stomp en masse when they're called a product of The University. But there is more of the Lit-major-reading trash in their music than they like to admit. "Druids are religious readers of Marvel Comics," they chortle. Their allusions are rife with mock-heroism: Carl Hauser calls himself "Thor." Tom Workman goes by the designation "Superbass." Steve Tindall fancies "Shifty Rodan." And Bill Tracy gets assorted titles, usually variations of "the Warp."

Any one of the Druids could have been the guy who slithered up Broadway one winter night, gripping his magic marker in one hand to write "Columbia Sucks" on the side of Ferris Booth Hall. Any one of them could have been the kid who wandered into the West End Bar and brushed past a mass of shiny round granny glasses, a jungle of striped ties, and a smoky forest of forgotten peacoats, to shout across the room at the nearest foamy, "I have discovered the ultimate psychedelic—man."

But the Druids are too busy playing rock 'n' roll to bother about such conventional pursuits of cool. Because rock 'n' roll means ultimate status. And the Druids are the top group on the upper West Side.

"I used to walk down the street," says Tom, "and they'd mutter: 'Hey—you one of the Rolling Stones?' Now they say 'You're one of the Druids, right?'"

The Druids have made it at Columbia. *Barnard Bulletin* did a piece on them, and the girls in tweed suits came scratching at their door. Then the agents arrived. Dave mimics: "Yous guys is really gud. Ya got a rekud contrak yet? We kud do a la'uh stuff fuh yuz." Friends in the business tapped them on the shoulder and whispered, "I want you to meet somebody who can make you boys a lot of money." There were a-and-r men who "deeply dig acid-rock," but also happen to have "every record Dion and the Belmonts ever made."

The Druids don't like to talk about The Business. They just like to get it. So they took a job at Ondine, an East Side discotheque. "At first they listened to us with half an ear," Dave recalls. "But you could tell they were impressed. Then, after a while they were nudging each other and we heard someone say—like, over the music—'dja heah that?'"

The Druids are resting up from 12 weeks at Ondine. They need it. The discotheque scene is different from fraternity row. It's out of the pot and into the cauldron.

"You get up on that stage, and you just have to close your eyes and forget who you are or why. You have a little back room to hibernate in between shows. When some greaser spills his drink on your pants or asks you to dance, when some tourist asks you

to play 'Auld Lang Syne,' you just have to concentrate on the music or blow your lunch."

You can almost see them, trapped in the bowels of the disco-monster; breathing fluorescent fire, emitting clouds of smoky mist, roaring, crashing, churning arms and torsos. The Druids, in the center of it all, try to make music. But playing three shows a night at a jammed discotheque is like being trapped in the belly of a bomb. The only consolation is the groupies. "It's like no society on earth," says Dave. "There's no leader or anything, because to be aggressive would make them less desirable."

"It's very weird," Tom declares, "to go back into a club and see the chicks who have sworn undying faith to the group making it with a guy playing the same instrument in a greasy band."

By acclamation, Ondine groupies are better than Barnard girls. "Ultimately," says Dave, "they're not as sticky. They don't look for anything meaningful in a relationship. And they know a hell of a lot more about hygiene."

The Druids are demi-masters of many demi-mondes. They are students. They are hippies. They are themselves. With the right water from the right can, Dave Budge's curling finger, Tracy's wiry hair, or Tom Workman's happy cool may become precious commodities. That's when it's good, when what you already are makes you special.

There are still hours in the studio, countless gigs at penny-ante wages, perhaps a crucial lay or two, and finally the crushing grind of playing B-group to the stars, which is like warming up the lions for the Christians. Even after all that, Tom may find himself a doctor. Dave may go back to the New School. And the others—now safely under the student umbrella—may soon find themselves facing Armageddon on Whitehall Street.

But now, the Druids know what they want out of rock 'n' roll: ease.

Tom: "I want to get to the point where I won't have to find a job. Nine hundred ninety-nine out of 1,000 people are unhappy in what they're doing. If I'm going to have to be unhappy, I'd rather have my choice."

Dave: "I'd like to reach the point where I don't have to say anything . . . where I didn't have to try to be hip. Two years ago, I

spent a lot of time doing that. But with five million-selling albums, you don't have to say anything. Your reputation goes ahead of you."

And Carl—modestly: "I'll have bodyguards to shoot people who try to harm my clothes."

The Druids. The top group on the upper West Side. Keep that in mind, John Lennon.

—THE VILLAGE VOICE, 1967

# ● SHANGO MICK ARRIVES

Shango, the African God of thunder, landed in New York City last Thursday afternoon.

He came wrapped in the steel body of a TWA jetliner, from the land of the new vinyl Shangos: London. At the airport that afternoon, worshipers stood tense and sweating along the open observation deck. Their hair lay plastered in streaks around their cheeks. Their binoculars were poised. Their Polaroid Swingers said "YES!"

The jet landed amid a churning blast of mechanical thunder. A portable staircase was fixed in place. Stewardesses and health officials arrived and departed. Finally, the Godheads: Charlie first—in brown. Then Bill and Keith. Then Brian, who removed his purple glasses to survey the scene and wiped them on his candy-cane blazer. Finally, Mick, smiling lamely, supported by the brass-button epaulets on his shoulder. The Gods descended and posed.

Their names are Bill Wyman, Charlie Watts, Keith Richard, Brian Jones, and Mick Jagger. All approximately twenty-one, and together the recipients of $8 million in hard popstar cash. Pete Hamill, a journalist who knows about such things, says they come on like an open switchblade. He means for real. We are not nice, but we are honest, says the image. We are not respectable, but we are genuine. We are evil, but cool.

Everybody here? Photographers, fashion models, lady editors, record executives, public-relations men, a few disheveled reporters,

27

and a stray groupie who is hustled off the field screaming "Keith—Keeeyth?"

We pass customs easily with a TWA man easing us through the baggage and embracing relatives. Now, out on the field, we watch the plane circle and descend. The party is small because King Faisal is landing today. The Stones may be rude but they don't insult Jews.

A PR man tells us what they're really like:

"Pigs. They're pigs."

A cop chimes in. "Last year a couple of girls broke through and touched them. We had to vaccinate them. You never saw so much smeared makeup. Jee-zuz."

A free-lance photographer says he'd rather be up in Yankee Stadium with the baseball players. "They show you some respect; they ask about the family."

And an airport porter advises: "They're down. Good luck. And remember the fifteen-foot business. Otherwise, you're contaminated."

ITEM FROM THE JAN. '66 ISSUE OF RAVE MAGAZINE: "Basically every pop singer is normal (despite what many say) and at times the hurdy-gurdy life of being continuously in the public eye is too much for anyone . . . Trying to be nice to everyone no matter what they say or do is sometimes too much."

FURTHER PERSPECTIVE FROM A FORMER PR MAN FOR THE STONES: "They go on the theory that a knock is a boost. No matter what they do, it's the Stones. If a clean-image group acted that way, they'd be finished. Suits, brawls, evictions—it's all part of the Stones' cool."

INSIGHT FROM A WRITER ON POP, AN ACQUAINTANCE, A FAN: "Mick belched in the middle of a press conference. It was the biggest belch in the world and he didn't say anything at all."

JAN CREMER TELLS ALL ABOUT BRIAN JONES: "I see Brian, all we talk about is pussy."

A large cardboard poster steals its way across the field. It's the cover of *Town and Country*—Stones meet society—blown up and transplanted to a 15-foot slab. Two fashion editors grasp the tribute and try to maneuver it into the customs area, where the Stones are being processed. But the cops stop them, so they park it on the hood of a limousine, where the boys will be sure to see it.

I wander over to customs. Handymen and porters gape and gawk from the windows. They are talking about those filthy, fruity kids inside. Since I'm wearing an official press card, the cops let me through. I meet the Rolling Stones. They are jumping around, hollering, scowling. Bill and Mick are laughing hysterically. Charlie is signing an autograph for a porter who has doubtless refused to move the group's instruments until a tissue is inscribed for his daughter.

Brian is standing alone. He turns and catches me snapping a contraband picture. He removes his shades, and those evil eyes begin to stare. It's a look I know from MacDougal Street. So, I stare back. Brian, why do they call you a god of destruction when you're just a kid jumping around making money and trouble? And Brian, are you ever frightened when those tiny feminine nails begin to scratch on your hotel door? And what's it like in those alone moments when the guitar is unplugged and the clothes come off and you're standing there in naked mufti with a woman?

We stare and I snap my picture and Brian puts his shades back on and scowls.

A FAN FROM MEMPHIS TELLS HIT PARADER MAGAZINE: "They've really homey type guys. I thought they were very nice and courteous, the very opposite of all the rumors I'd heard because everyone told me they were gonna be real rude and wouldn't want to talk to me."

A BRITISH JOURNALIST SAYS: "Talking to the Stones is like going to the dentist. A few 'fag gear whacks' and a little 'in' patter which you cannot possibly share reduce reporters to stuttering, embarrassed heaps."

NEW YORK, June 24—The Rolling Stones, prominent British pop-music singing group, held an informal press reception on their

rented yacht, Sea Panther, today. The five musicians are being quartered on the 112-foot craft during their current American tour because hotel officials have refused to grant them reservations. They are currently suing 14 New York hotels in the dispute.

The reception began as the yacht departed from the 79th Street Boat Basin. All of the Stones were present, and their manager, Andrew Loog Oldham, enthusiastically held forth amid a cluster of reporters. A buffet luncheon was served.

The group was splendidly attired in their distinctive style. Mick Jagger, lead vocalist, wore a striped double-breasted blazer and white bell-bottom slacks. Song writer Keith Richard wore an epaulet shirt and red suede boots. And guitarist Brian Jones placed a button, "Sex is here to stay," on the fly of his white, wide-wale corduroys.

A LYRICAL INTERLUDE: "You're the kind of person you meet at certain dismal dull affairs. You say how the crowd is much too loud running up and down the stairs. Well it seems to me that you have sinned too much in too few years. And though you try you just can't hide. Your eyes are filled with tears."

—*Nineteenth Nervous Breakdown*
by JAGGER AND RICHARD

The motors churn and the yacht begins to move. Mick says: "It's 95 out and you'd never know it here." Charlie says: "Don't let those photographers make you nervous; ask your questions." Keith says efforts to censor rock songs because of their subject is: "Typical American prudery." Brian says· "The next thing in pop won't happen for another three years."

The press meets/versus the Rolling Stones. A starry-eyed reporter for the New York *Post* follows Oldham around, scrawling dutifully on a worn pad. Those ladies from *Town and Country* are back with their publicity blowup. The boys pose and the ladies smile, their jobs secure until the next pop group comes to town. WMCA goodguys Gary Stevens, in a blue pin stripe suit, chortles: "Hey, Keith Baby, how about we do a tape? We do a tape, huh?" So Keith smiles lamely and says: "Sure, Gary." And Charlie sits, yawns, and smokes cigarettes.

Meanwhile, Mick is responding to a question. "What's the difference between the Stones and the Beatles?"

"There are five of us and four of them."

Brian stares at the passing Statue of Liberty, pulls out a red handkerchief, and waves it in the general direction of the bronze lady.

"Who are more uncooperative, Brian? British or American journalists?"

"We're the ones who are uncooperative, right mate?"

THE ART DIRECTOR OF A FAN MAGAZINE GASPS AT BRIAN JONES' BEHAVIOR: "I was taking pictures of him at a discotheque and he walked right up to me, stuck out his chest, and said: 'I wouldn't do that again, mate.' I really thought he was going to hit me."

A POP WRITER COMPARES THE OLD AND NEW STONES: "I think now there's a feeling of—don't touch me, I'm a Rolling Stone. Even their manager is so hung up on himself, it's unbelievable. And Mick is a hippy in the true sense of the word. When someone says something honest, he goes blank. He can't relate to honesty."

I am sitting next to Mick. I consider the proper approach. With Brian it's easy; all you have to do is snap. With Charles and Bill, be friendly. With Keith, be musically knowledgeable. With their manager, build up your paper's circulation.

But Mick defies approach. The others are shorter, pudgier, softer than they sound on record. But Mick really looks like a Shango. A while ago, he was hospitalized suffering from a "nervous exhaustion." Now you observe him smiling, chatting, responding. You watch him "circulate." You notice his tired grin, his oval eyes and sagging lips; his yachtsman's jacket is an irony. You want to ask: "Mick, how the hell are you going to manage concerts in 29 cities in 27 days?" You want to say: "Mick, tell me about payola. About under-assistant West Coast promo-men. How does $8 million feel? Does Ed Sullivan have bad breath?" But you can't do that at a press reception, on a yacht circling Manhattan Island. You want to touch Mick Jagger? You can't even come close.

So, pen poised, eyes shining, you state lamely: "I want to do a

piece about the reality of being a Rolling Stone." And Mick Jagger smiles. "The reality of being me? It's nasty today."

JAN CREMER ELABORATES ON GROUPIES: "You go on stage. You do your work. You go home. But every night, fifty ugly-looking girls are banging on your door. Well, the first night, you think it's funny. The second night you say, 'Boy, I'm getting popular." But by the third night, you want to say, 'Fuck off, all.' "

LYRICAL DIVERSION AND PREGNANT PAUSE:

> When I'm riding round the world
> And I'm doing this and I'm signing that
> And I'm trying to make some girl
> Who tells me, baby better come back
> Maybe next week
> Can't you see I'm on a losing streak!

Ashore, 200 girls shriek as the Rolling Stones leave their yacht. Six policemen cordon off a route to the underground garage where the limousine is parked, doors ajar. The Stones, braced for a riot, walk into the waiting police arms, but the girls are persistent and experienced. They break the lines and rush the group. The Stones scurry madly into the cavernous garage. Everyone makes it except Brian who is engulfed in lips and fingernails. A shrieking hand pulls his hair. Something snags his lip. Five girls clutch at his jacket and pants. Twilight of the gods. Brian is pale and helpless. Sacrificial wailing. The reporters form a flying wedge and begin to pull the fans from Brian's back. Finally he climbs inside, while a girl screams after him: "I got a thread." The car takes off, but not before the groupies throw themselves over the hood kamikaze style. The garage explodes in shrieks of brakes and ecstasy. Real tears are shed. Hands are quivering. Hair is thrown wildly as the car pulls away.

Outside, an African sun shines over the Sea Panther. Muffled sound of drumbeats from the river. Burst of thunder from the motors. And a girl with merging freckles asks: "Dijuh touch him? Dijuh touch Mick Jagger?"

—THE VILLAGE VOICE, 1966

# THE LOVIN' SPOONFUL: SO, WHO BELIEVES IN MAGIC?

It starts in the lobby of the Sheraton Chicago when, amid all that polite plastic and gilded glass, the doors of the Grand Ballroom swing open, pouring out a phalanx of clapping, chanting Hassidic Jews.

It's a wedding. The whole totem and taboo is there, rabbis in fur-rimmed hats, mothers in organza togas, kids in black stovepipe uniforms, with sideburns curled cautiously around their ears.

The bride and groom walk stiffly, like cake statues. A bellboy drops a handful of keys in surprise. Chicago matrons and two-button businessmen gawk in dismay as the whole happening crosses the lobby.

On the other side, these four guys are lounging against a staircase in longhaired striped shirt roundglasshiphugger dirty booted uniforms. They are not at all astonished at witnessing such a wedding in such a lobby; it reads like part of their act. The bride gazes absently over her shoulder as she is whisked by. The owlish guy on the stairs, with the super sideburns and round wire glasses, smiles at her and waves hello with his chin.

It blows her mind utterly. She blushes, and whispers to her husband, "That's John Sebastian. The Lovin' Spoonful."

So it starts. The Spoonful are in town for two concerts at Chicago's McCormick Place Theater. They are tired. Groups on tour are always tired. Just in from Houston in their private plane,

shaggy and unshaven, they confront a hazy, Brooklynesque Chicago from within two rented cars. Guys driving home from work make faces at Zal Yanovsky, who makes faces back without even trying. Young formica marrieds double back for a look. Joe Butler gazes at the silent bobbing heads as though he were watching from underwater; he knows what they are saying by heart: "That kid with the big nose looks like some kind of Arab." Truck drivers whistle at Steve Boone, who is too busy trying to get his stomach off the plane to notice. And John Sebastian gazes at the approaching skyline and thinks ahead three hours when he will be dodging a panting, throbbing pack of girls.

Sebastian isn't made for the idol game. He smiles in corners, but in crowds he buttons himself up like a knapsack, straps his mind onto his shoulders, and stalks away. A transplanted New Yorker, he endured adolescence, and discovered the Village when he went to school there (a year and a half at NYU as an Italian major, because he knew the language already). He learned to play the harmonica because his father is a virtuoso. As Lightning Hopkin's water boy, he developed a purist's sense of funk. Even the group's name comes from a Mississippi John Hurt song, "Coffee Blues": "I love my baby by the lovin' spoonful."

When Sebastian found Nashville rock 'n' roll, he began to write in spurts—on subways, in restaurants, in bed. At first, you couldn't touch his songs with a ten-foot falsetto. Now they talk about the Sebastian sound as though its creator were the mythical turtle-god, carrying the world of pop music on his back.

By now, "Daydream" has had more cover versions than the Bible. Sebastian's ode to lazy contemplation has been lacquered, powdered, and given a crew cut. Respectably stringed-up, it reaches every commuter on the Long Island Expressway. In brassy drag, it makes the cocktail-party circuit. And, as naked melody, it has become music by which to buy frozen meat.

The Lovin' Spoonful have emerged as standard-bearers, hip prophets, the real thing. West Coast jazz critic Ralph Gleason claims: "They're the best group in the U.S. I'm glad to be alive at a time when I can hear them." *Newsweek* observes: "They chant the eternal verities of all popular music—from psalms to Sinatra." And

*The New York Times* concludes that their work is "timeless, traditional, yet modern, alive with something for all generations."

All of which makes John Sebastian smile that gee-I'm-a-poet
grin and observe: "Well, all that ready praise makes creating very
easy. A month after I've written something, it gets heard and
evaluated. Whenever I do, I get."

Sebastian coined the term "good-time music" to describe his
sound. It begins squarely in the jug-band tradition, then wavers
delicately between ragtime and funky blues, and finally ends up on
its own, still rock 'n' roll, but something more; something brandy-
warm, doghonest, moonpure.

"Good-time music" won't respond to terse analysis. Sober con-
clusions about the complexities involved (i.e. subtle lyric scan,
bubbling calliope effects, clinging harpwork, wispy falsetto backing,
and all those old-timey changes) leave the feeling untouched. It
won't stand still long enough to be classified. That horrible writer's
moment of non-description leaves two possibilities. I present both:

A. Effect is maintained by inclusion of humorous instrumental
variance, unobtrusive lyric, and image-sequence, intricate harmonics, and intensively softened vocal pattern.

B. Tonight's audience opened up like speed-filmed flowers. In
"Rain on the Roof," the sound hit solid like a Walt Disney real-life
adventure, with a baby deer standing in the high grass, feet
wobbling, nose shiny wet. When the Spoonful sang "Daydream,"
the audience went furry. . . .

But the last word on "good-time music" comes from the fans.
Every combo inspires a crush of thumping teen libidos, but the
Lovin' Spoonful groupie reaches out, struggling with pimpled
sexuality, and the music reaches in—way in.

"Dear John," she writes: "Watching the river glide along in the
woods behind my grandmother's farm reminds me of your singing."

"By now you're probably wondering—is she deep?"

"Dear Zal: Do you like radishes? For some strange reason, you
remind me of a radish. Joe reminds me of lettuce because he's
crispy."

"Mostly, in a weird little way, I'm grateful to you. Would you
understand if once in a while you felt low and heard 'thump . .
boom . . . . blummmmm . . . you didn't have to be so nice.' "

"John, you must be a pretty witty character. Do you happen to know what your IQ is?"

"About Zal—is he German or just what is he if you know what I mean?"

"Please Zal, don't be insulted by all those Jew jokes. We love the Jews, honest."

"What a perfectly comfortable name John Benson Sebastian is."

"Dear Spoonful—love each other. Love me too, if you have room."

There is Tina, who is 14, but looks and sounds "menopausal." She is deeply in love with Zalman . . . spiritually, of course. There is Sybil, turgid and Wagnerian. The fan-club hint-book notes: "Try to be encouraging." There is the girl from Texas who is trying to buy the Spoons an elephant.

And there are Abigail and Honey, both 16, who have slipped past the guards and are standing in the corridor of the Chicago Sheraton, waiting to touch the Lovin' Spoonful. Honey says: "I love the lyrics . . . their voices are so soft." Abigail nervously twirls the bow of her leather purse. Her cheeks flush teenie-pink. She nibbles on the end of her hair. "They're the greatest group there is," she whispers. "Their music is so . . . real."

Fifteen floors below, Zalman Yanovsky has reached the lobby unmolested in his knee-length fun-fur. Everyone tells him he has missed the wedding of the century. A ruffle-bloused matron lifts her bifocals, then jolts back into an escalator going up. Zal smiles back, through drooping eyes.

"I don't know any frenzy of the business," he says. "I mean I like to explore my own possibilities."

And John goes home. "When the hassles start, I get cooled out with my wife, and our surroundings. There's come to be a lot of warmth in my house that seems to assuage the wounds."

In the distance, the shouting starts. Outside the hotel, the kids are bunched around the rented limousines—pea-coated, high-booted, bell-bottomed. Let them get too close and they'll rip you apart like a dog with a stuffed doll in his teeth. Stand within tossing distance and they'll pelt you with jellybeans that feel like cobble-stones, or paper rockets that knick like darts. They throw scrawled propositions. They throw bears, in honor of Pooh. They throw silver

spoons. They throw wire glasses. Once they hit Joe on the head with a block of hashish, but that was in Berkeley.

All together now—Steve and Joe and John with Laurie and Joe's girl and furry Zal and the road managers race down the staircase like a buffalo stampede (some lady blurts—"My god, they've got a gorilla"), make a flying wedge through the revolving door, and past the kiddie crush. They make it unscarred into the car and race toward McCormick Place preceded by 1500 pounds of equipment in sixty pieces of luggage. All along the way, there is that distant echo of screaming. Zal is making faces at a gesturing couple. Joe is biting a hangnail. Steve is deflating his shoulders. John is whispering to his wife, Laurie. Everyone is scared shitless. It is usually like this in a strange town before a concert.

"Sometimes now when I see a number is blown, I don't let it blow me for the rest of the night," says Joe. "But only sometimes."

"When you go on stage saying you have to be funny all the time, you lose spontaneity," says John. "We avoid that by doing a lousy show sometimes."

Zal is pissed off because the group can't really play most of the material from their new album onstage yet. He moves in spurts— hand to eye, foot to knee, mouth open for a series of fuck-the-world put-downs. "One or two shitty numbers sets the pace," he warns. "The only way to get out of it is to stop trying to get out of it." He lurches forward and back in his seat, buried in fur and hair. "Sort of like Zen."

The car veers off the road toward an underground stage entrance masquerading as a garage. Zal warns: "Close your windows."

The screeching sound that has remained in the background as a constant din, grows louder. A girl brandishing a vinyl umbrella is pointing at the approaching limousines. Two sentries—blondes in granny dresses—signal wildly. They are all over the cars in no time, charging the door, clutching the fenders, banging on the windows. Notice me . . . smile at me . . . rub me . . . Zally . . . Zal.

He opens his eyes only after the garage door slams shut. Upstairs, the Blues Magoos are earning their share of the gate. Both groups call the Night Owl home, but the Magoos, in eclectic phosphorescence, are the psychedelic sound. Backstage, Zal sheds his fur and picks up his guitar. Joe scrawls tonight's program on his palm.

Steve tries turning down the volume on the speaker which broadcasts cues into every dressing room. John sits curled around his autoharp, strumming, tuning, thinking. Tired.

There are thirty minutes left to rehearse. But a local disc jockey has other ideas. He pops backstage to greet the evening's stars. He approaches Joe, who looks glassy-eyed over his shoulder. "How about we do a little tape, baby, okay?" And then he asks Joe to define "sex appeal."

"Anything that makes me think of it," Joe says.

The D.J. laughs an obscene-to-say-that-on-the-air giggle and gives Joe the high sign. In dressing room one, John is still strumming.

"Journalists aren't in their medium with us," he observes. "They come on hostile because of their own defense mechanisms."

In walks the D.J. How about we do a little tape, John baby? John baby shrugs. He asks his question. Sebastian squirms.

"C'mon, define sex appeal."

"Haven't you got another question?"

"That's the only one, baby."

"I don't want to answer that."

"Just for fun, man, just for fun. All kinds of people do this sort of thing for us and. . . ."

". . . another question. . . ."

". . . you know, everyone has something to say on. . . ."

". . . nothing. . . ."

". . . sex appeal, so how about it, John? Baby?"

"No." The D.J. shuts off his tape recorder. A momentary glare passes between the two men. The dimple-smile fades. Punk-faggot-beatnik Sebastian, sitting there, knees doubled over an autoharp. "Whatsamadder, John?" "Just funning," he gulps. Snotnose bastard. He shrugs his shoulders. Prick. He slams the door. John goes back to his music.

On stage, among the red and green and purple lights, Sebastian is still wrapped around his harp. Butler grimaces over his drums. Boone stands off to the side, caressing his bass. And Zally stretches his rubberface, blowing a red clown's horn into the effect. Zally the folk-hero. Lived in a laundromat. Quit school at 16, and split to Israel. Master of the put on put-on. He plays and sings a mean

storm. Says he likes to guzzle potato soup, Canadian bacon, Chinese food, and bialys with cream cheese. His ideal groupie is "a schwartze with an overbite and a big, juicy snatch." He enters a room like an ugly kid out to show the world he's around. On the street in Oldtown, he shakes everything up in his fur. When they squeal "that's Zally," he laughs-smirks: cut that out . . . harder, harder. He calls Joe fatty and complains: "He's the son of an Irish cop and he smells like cabbage." Everybody cracks up at the Zally joke except Zally. He jabs quickly and quietly, and then retreats to laugh at the blood.

But Zal is no fake. On stage, he is as obstinately unpredictable as off. "I don't like to be funny all the time," he says. "Sometimes I go out of my way to be nasty, just for the principle." Even nasty, he is part of the Lovin' Spoonful magic.

Because that's what Good Time Music is all about. The magic of not-quite-boys singing at almost-men, and making it all sound loving. Ask the kids. The Spoonful write and sing the best psychedelic music around. All that raucous acid-rock, all that diarrhetic lighting, all that raga-religiosity miss the point.

The Lovin' Spoonful are everybody's legendary high. They warm you slowly from the bottom. They bubble like smoke inside your lungs. They make you giggle. They blow your mind. They let you down easy. They leave you feeling sleepy-good.

—THE VILLAGE VOICE, 1966

# ● MORE MYSTERIOSO, MR. KRAMER

John Kramer—songwriter, market-research coder, musician, sales-man of men's socks, folk-singer, owner of a Chicago mutt named Micky, former owner of a New York poodle named Dildo, and superstar-to-be—is 15 minutes late.

He was to begin an over-dubbing session on his first record at 11 P.M. His label is Columbia—the most powerful in the country. After three years in New York at odd jobs and unemployment ("I'm selective about jobs; I select which days I want to work"), Sunbeam Music signed him. Now it pays $150 a month for John to sit home and write songs. His music is soft and melodic. His lyrics are ironic rather than tragic. While his tone is often satiric, his subject matter is almost always the despair of being alone and being neglected. The genre is more difficult to describe. Look straight at his music and it's folk. Listen closely and it's ragtime. Blink your eye, and it becomes rock 'n' roll behind your back.

John Kramer has always been nervous about recording. Pills don't help. They don't prevent the hoarseness and sore throat which always seem to attack him when he is due to record. Cough medicine doesn't do any good. The cracking voice is a sure sign that John has a session coming up, as are headaches, insomnia, diarrhea, an intense craving for Pepsi Cola, and any number of symptoms. Everyone kids about getting the "big break," but when it comes, everything is dead serious. John Kramer wants, more than anything

else in this world, to be a superstar. Columbia Records can make him that, or ignore him. So Columbia makes him nervous.

We meet at the recording studio, a converted church on the East Side. John is dressed in a coffee-colored summer suit. A smile; a friendly interview-type handshake. He rings the nightbell. No answer. He runs around the corner to call in, but the telephone is broken, so he loses his last dime. Back at the church, he slams at the bell and begs it to answer. Thirty minutes late, and only an echo. No one home. Shit.

"Hop into a cab. It's in the big building on 52nd and Sixth."

John Kramer slumps into his seat, then jumps erect with a glance at his watch; 11:45 P.M. "They'll blame me; I know they will! Everybody knows where these things are but me. Columbia owns the whole city."

Three hangnails come off in John's mouth and are quickly digested. The taxi cruises leisurely past 42nd Street.

"They want me to change my name," John reports. "First I figured—Harry Pileburger. The ethnic approach. Then, John Oliver—sounds English . . . the Crispian-Saint-French-Fry bit."

We stop for a light.

"How does Arthur Nouveau hit you?" John asks.

"How about Seashell and Carbuncle?" I inquire. But the cab has stopped and John bounds ahead. We have arrived at the sparkling monument to CBS Inc. We march through the immense black demi-columns, and into the controlled climate of an office building. We race into an elevator in a frantic search for Recording Studio A. We career past rows of offices and reception desks. Each department looks like an airport waiting room; pop and op adorn the walls. We enter Studio A, faced with a hostile row of screens and three very grim looking men. We have wandered by mistake into Studio A WCBS Radio, and are summarily thrown out. Out into the street for a trot over to Broadway, where still another Columbia edifice stands. John says, "My throat feels like a furnace."

Columbia's Tin Pan Alley studio. Enter John Kramer—one hour late, despite warnings from his agent about being on time. Still muttering "They're going to blame me," he rings for the elevator. A

porter claims it's locked. We race around the block and enter through an alley which smells of chop suey. Up four flights of sweating stairs and into a door marked, at last, Studio A.

John Kramer is a Chicago boy. At 12 he played cymbals for the American Legion Marching Drum and Bugle Corps. At 12½, he broke his nose between two smashing cymbals. John's parents and grandmother still live in an old house on the Near North Side. The gas furnace in their living room explodes into action every so often, covering the walls with a blue glow and emitting a sound of roasting popcorn. Hillbillies live upstairs.

Today John lives in Brooklyn Heights—an inveterate New Yorker. His instruments, his stuffed owl named Louise, and his collage of Jean Harlow and Ringo adorn the walls. John's A and R man at Columbia is Howard Roberts. He is a pro, you can tell that from his monograms. Three men are present with Howard in the studio. One will modulate the pre-recorded music over which John will sing. One will work the decibel knobs, and one, a friend, will comment on the soul.

"John, you're late."

He sits alone in the studio. They have turned out the lights and placed him behind an immense acoustical screen. Instruments are scattered around the room. The ceiling is covered with thick sound-proof tiles.

John takes off his tie and shoes, loosens his belt, and gulps water. Every nervous swallow is audible in the control booth. John is recording his first single, an up-tempo number called "The Moving Finger Writes." Columbia has added an Oriental Gypsy flavored background to his lyrics. The Sonny-and-Cher bag.

For the first three takes, his voice is hoarse and hesitant. Howard cuts in. "This is your first statement to the world and it has to be strong and dramatic. These are your words—it's your sound. I don't care how much ham you have to use. Let the world know you're here and now. Let them know you count."

Howard's pep-talk registers. By take number eight, John's voice is strong. His new-found power shakes the control booth. By the 10th take, they are down to minor points. "Get a little cry into

that phrase," says Howard. From the background, Howard's friend mouths the lyrics with a pained and furrowed brow.

"They expect soul from me?" John asks. "I'm from the Midwest."

It is 1 A.M., so nobody laughs. Minor flubs on the next two takes bring the total to 15. Howard announces, "This will be it, John."

The music begins. There is Chicago, and those forgotten engagements with the Steele Singers, three clean-cut folk musicians who toured the country as part of a hootenanny package and did commercials for Orange Crush. There is New York City—mooched meals, a room at the YMCA, living with friends in the Bronx, and borrowing movie money. Promises from another record company don't pan out, and all those smiling faces ask "But what do you *do*, John?"

What he does is entertain. Now, there is nothing left to do but sing. In that soundproof cavern is everything that John Kramer has ever wanted. He pats the microphone tenderly. Inside are current and velocity—and making it.

Take 15 is over. Howard's friend is still mouthing lyrics. The man at the knob lights his eighth cigarette. John is chewing on the remnant of his last whole fingernail.

A critic's silence. Howard opens his eyes and whispers, groans, implores, "More mysterioso."

Back into the booth for another try. If John Kramer makes it, he will be able to hire fingernails to bite on. But at 3 A.M., he is down to the last cuticle.

"Cue me, Howard."

—THE VILLAGE VOICE, 1966

# II
# PERSONNEL

# ● BEAUTIFUL CREEP

And the child on whose shoulders I stand,
whose longing I purged
with public, kingly discipline,
today I bring him back
to languish forever
not in confession or biography,
but where he flourished,
growing sly and hairy.

—LEONARD COHEN

("*The Flowers That I Left in the Ground*") *

An elevator man with hairy hands grumbles "shit" as he takes me up. It is a massive midtown hotel, in steep decline. The corridors are long and lit occasionally, like a cardboard coal mine. Humid ladies in black lace seem to peer from every transom, and old men with their backs turned lurk in every shadowy corner. There is a smell of stale cigars, or is it piss? I knock politely on a wafer-thin door, and wait.

Finally it opens, and Leonard Cohen, Canada's most acclaimed young poet and novelist, offers a seat and some coffee. He has been listening to a tape of the half-completed album on which he will

* Leonard Cohen, *Selected Poems 1956-1968*. Copyright in all countries of the International Copyright Union. All rights reserved. Reprinted by permission of The Viking Press, Inc.

47

soon make his debut as a pop star (a year ago that would have given even me pause, but not today, when Leonard Bernstein picks the hits and the *Partisan Review* talks about "Learning from the Beatles"). His verse—collected in slim volumes perfect for pressing roses—is so unabashedly romantic that it sits among my New Directions paperbacks like some later-day Ossian.

> With Annie gone
> Whose eyes to compare
> With the morning sun?
>
> Not that I did compare,
> But I do compare
> Now that she's gone.*
>
> ("*For Anne*")

No wonder Allen Ginsberg huffed out of a meeting with Leonard Cohen muttering, "This place looks like a ballet set." There is a shameless agility to those leaps and conceits, which seems ethereal next to the bugaloo of modern verse.

But Leonard Cohen is a Visceral Romantic and he can hit you unawares because his emotions are recollected in anything but tranquility. He suffers gloriously in every couplet. Even his moments of ecstasy seem predicated on hours of refined despair. Leonard does not rant; he whispers hell and you must strain to hear his agony.

Today he faces me across a hotel room with the sun shining second hand in the windows down the block. The drapes are as florid as his verse. In fact, the room could be the set for most of his poems. The bedspread is faded, and you can hear the toilet. Atop the bureau is a seashell ashtray embossed with Miami palm trees. To this pasteboard Chappaqua Leonard Cohen has added only a madonna decal for the mirror and a terrible cold.

His front pockets bulge with tissues and Sucrets. The cold seems appropriate; his nose aches to be filled anyway. It is a huge nose, etched by some melancholy woodcarver into the hollows of his cheeks. He wipes it and wheezes gently as we hear a tape of his song "Teachers."

* Cohen, *Selected Poems*.

Though he claims he has always written with a typewriter for a guitar ("I sometimes see myself in the Court of Ferdinand, singing my songs to girls over a lute"), Leonard Cohen has been spending this past year or so creating lyrics with real melodies. He made his pop debut recently as Judy Collins' beautiful person. Her choice was inspired; Leonard Cohen has written her best material—songs of love and torment powerful enough to be fairy tales.

"I think my album is going to be very spotty and undistinguished," he says in greeting. His eyes sag like two worn breasts. "I blame this on my total unfamiliarity with the recording studio. They tried to make my songs into music. I got put down all the time." He sits back on his bed, folds his hands in his lap, and lets his voice fade into an echo of itself: "It was a continual struggle . . . continual . . . they wanted to put me in bags. I thought I was going to . . . crack up."

He is modestly addicted to cracking up. References to breakdowns past and future dot his conversation. He seems to judge periods in his life by his failure to cope with them. His favorite words—or those he uses most frequently—are "wiped out" and "bewildered."

"When you get wiped out—and it does happen in one's life—that's the moment . . . the REAL moment. Around 30 or 35 is the traditional age for the suicide of the poet, did you know? That's the age when you finally understand that the universe does not succumb to your command."

That moment magnified into theme, is the chief concern of his major novel, *Beautiful Losers*. It is a multisexual love story, ecstatically lyric like his poems, but deeply committed as prose to expressing its theme through an accumulation of detail. Its protagonist, a petty researcher, is victimized by the love of his wife and of his best friend. They control his life, soothe him, fuck him, teach him, cuckold him, and ultimately destroy him. Their triangle, joined on all sides, is further complicated by Catherine Tekakwitha, an Indian saint who fixes herself in the protagonist's consciousness as an extension of his wife (also an Indian) and his own suffering. Martyred by the suicides of both his lover-tormentors, our hero is left to ponder the moral of Catherine's life: suffering is madness, but it is also the sacred ground where Man encounters God. That

we are all fated to walk this ground is Leonard Cohen's message.
To embrace that agony of communion is to live with grace.

> It begins with your family,
> But soon it comes round to your soul.
> Well, I've been where you're hanging
> I think I can see where you're pinned
> When you're not feeling holy
> Your loneliness says that you've sinned.

*("Sisters of Mercy")*

He was born in Montreal to a wealthy Jewish family. "I had a
very Messianic childhood," he recalls. "I was told I was a descend-
ant of Aaron, the high priest. My parents actually thought we
were Cohenim—the real thing. I was expected to grow into man-
hood leading other men."

He led himself through McGill, where he studied literature with
Oxonian aplomb. A professor published a volume of his poetry on
the University press, and Leonard Cohen became a writer. It was,
he insists, "as accidental as that."

Because with any choice, he would have become a revolutionary.
But he approached radicalism with a bad cold, and a thorough
knowledge of the Tonette. Though the Montreal Communists
fascinated him with their paranoia and their certainty, he was less
than embraced by his chosen confreres. "They saw me as a symbol
of the decline of the enemy," he recalls. "I never had that heroic
revolutionary look. There was a certain openshirted quality I
could never duplicate. I always looked different, maybe because my
folks owned a clothing factory."

Today he wears poet's gray, and a soft worker's hat hangs on his
closet door. He is getting old; the trousers of his cuffs are sta-
press-rolled. He watches you jot that down in the middle of a
point about politics and you wonder if he knows you plan to use it.

"I'm not a writer coming to music in the twilight of his youth," he
says suddenly. You look up. He begins to discuss the rock scene,
then and now. Once, he thought Elvis Presley the first American
singer of genius. Once, he played a Ray Charles record till it warped
in the sun. Once, he thought of himself as Bob Dylan's ancestor.
"It wasn't his originality which first impressed me, but his famili-

arity. He was like a person out of my books, singing to the real guitar. Dylan was what I'd always meant by the poet—someone about whom the word was never used."

Until a short time ago, Leonard Cohen had never heard Dylan. He has spent much of the past seven years in a cottage on Hydra, Greece. He still returns there regularly for replenishment, the way F. Scott Fitzgerald's heroes go back to the Midwest. It keeps him from making too many scenes outside himself; that seems to be the scene he can make best.

> Anyhow you fed her 5 McKewan Ales,
> took her to your room, put the right records on,
> and in an hour or two it was done.
> I know all about passion and honour
> but unfortunately, this had really nothing to do with either:
> oh there was passion I'm only too sure
> and even a little honour
> but the important thing was to cuckold Leonard Cohen. . . .
> I like that line because it's got my name in it.*
>
> *("The Cuckold's Song")*

"I wrote 'Beautiful Losers' on Hydra, when I'd thought of myself as a loser. I was wiped out; I didn't like my life. I vowed I would just fill the pages with black or kill myself. After the book was over, I fasted for ten days and flipped out completely. It was my wildest trip. I hallucinated for a week. They took me to a hosptial in Hydra. One afternoon, the whole sky was black with storks. They alighted on all the churches and left in the morning . . . and I was better. Then, I decided to go to Nashville and become a song writer."

He came to New York instead, thanks to a lady who is now his manager. And here he is—slaving over the songs he calls "Eastern-Country-laments," trying to make them sound the way they read. Things are happening for Leonard Cohen. "Suzanne," his best-known lyric, made the charts on a vacuous version by Noel Harrison. Two recent compositions appear on the latest Judy Collins album. And Buffy Sainte Marie will include the selections from "Beautiful Losers" on her next LP. Sometimes the two visit Saint Patrick's, where there is a bas-relief of Catherine Tekakwitha on one of the Cathedral doors. Buffy puts daisies in the statue's hair.

* Cohen, *Selected Poems.*

"She sees the suffering in Catherine," he explains. "She feels the thumping on the sky."

If his forthcoming album is a good one, Leonard Cohen may well become one of history's odder choices for pop stardom. But the men we deem to worship are never ordinary; that is the one passion they must guard against. If the time is ripe for a guru with a cold in the ego, Leonard Cohen's modest agony will stand him in good stead.

"My songs are strangely romantic," he admits, "but so are the kids. I somehow feel that I have always waited for this generation." He pulls out a letter from a young girl who wonders over his unremitting despair. He frightens her because she senses that he has achieved an understanding of life, but he is sad despite it. She prays that the comprehension she seeks will not bring her such misery. She prays for him, and for herself, that he is really blind. And she ends by calling Leonard Cohen a "beautiful creep."

Real tears form in the corners of his eyes, but modestly they do not flow. He sighs for real. "That's what I am—a beautiful creep." He excuses himself and you grab for the letter when he is gone. That too is real.

Beautiful creep! You can't help hearing him in the toilet; he pisses in quick panting spurts. You want to put him to bed with hot milk and butter, turn up the vaporizer, and kiss him good night.

> And you want to travel with him
> And you want to travel blind
> And you think maybe you'll trust him
> For he's touched your perfect body with his mind.*
>
> ("*Suzanne*")

—THE VILLAGE VOICE, 1967

* © 1966 by Project Seven Music.

# ● NEXT YEAR IN
# SAN FRANCISCO

Tonight's crowd ambles languidly across the floor of Philadelphia's Electric Factory, a huge garage turned psychedelic playground. Mostly, they are straight kids come to gape at the hippies and fathom the Now. Ten years ago, they would have preened their pompadours before the cameras on American Bandstand. Today, they steal furtive drags on filter-tip cigarettes trying to look high. With coiled springs behind their eyes, they flash stiff South-Phillie grins at any chick who looks like she might go down. They've all had their palms read by the Wizard in the balcony, and their faces painted in the adjacent boutique. Now they stand like limp meringue, watching a local group called Edison's Electric Machine belt warm-up jive.

A real deathscene. Not a pleasant sight for Janis Joplin, who peers through a crack in the dressing room door, and scowls: "Oh shit. It's dead out there. We'll never be able to get into those kids. Want to see death? Take a look out there. You ever played Philadelphia? No, of course not. You don't *play* anywhere."

When Janis scowls, her whole face closes up around her mouth and even her eyelashes seem to frown. You could say she gets nervous before a set. The other members of Big Brother and the Holding Company sit guzzling beer, trying on beads, and hassling their road manager. But Janis stalks around the tiny room, her fingers drumming against a tabletop. She sips hot tea from a styro-

53

foam cup. She talks in gasps, and between sentences, she belts a swig of Southern Comfort, her trademark. Tonight, a knowing admirer has graced her dressing room with a fifth, in lieu of flowers. "I don't drink anything on the rocks," she explains. "Cold is bad for my throat. So, it's always straight or in tea. Tastes like orange petals in tea. I usually get about a pint and a half down me, when I'm performing. Any more, I start to nod out."

Now the B-group files in, dripping sweat. The lead singer gingerly places his guitar in its plush casket and peels off an imitation-brocade jacket, sweatshirt, pullover, and drenched undershirt. "Why do you wear all that clothing it it's so hot out there?" Janis asks.

"Because I'm freaky." And the door opens again to admit a fully-attired gorilla with rubber hands and feet. Janis glances briefly at the ground to make sure that it's still there, and then she offers the gorilla some booze and he lifts his mask to accept. His name is Gary the Gorilla, and Janis digs that, so she gives him her bottle to hold during the group's set and follows Peter the bassman through the door, while the crowd shouts for music. Gary unzips his belly and passes his feet around, and the lead singer of Edison's Electric Machine examines a rip in his brocade, consoling himself with the B-group's prayer: Next Year In San Francisco.

I first met them last year in San Francisco. In a ranch house with an unobstructed view of tickytack. They were assembled for an interview on Hippy-culture, and I began with a nervous question about turning on. In answer, somebody lit up and soon the floor was hugging-warm. I glanced down at my notes as though they had become hieroglyphics (which, it later turned out, they had). When it was time to split, and everyone had boarded a paisley hearse, I muttered something like: "We shouldn't be interviewed. We should be friends." And the car drove away laughing, with long hair flying from every window.

This summer, there will be 20,000 yelpers on Haight Street, hoping to get discovered, like Janis, in some psychedelic Schwab's. But I'm afraid Big Brother and the Holding Company is the last of the great San Francisco bands. With new groups trying on serious music like a training bra, they are a glorious throwback to a time

when the primary aim in rock was "to get people moving"—nothing more or less. They were nurtured in the roots of the Hip renaissance (played the Trips Festival and the first productions of the Family Dog; jammed together in a big house at 1090 Page Street, a mecca for musicians back when the only interested talent scouts were cops). Now they are its most fragrant late-summer blossom.

In 1961, Janis and Chett Holmes (proprietor of the Family Dog) hitchhiked west. They were anonymous freaks then, newly plucked from Texas topsoil and still green.

"What were the two of you like then, Janis?"

"Oh—younger."

"How were you different from today?"

"We were . . . ummm . . . just interested in being beatniks then. Now, we've got responsibilities, and I guess you could say, ambition."

She was born in Port Arthur, Texas, in 1943. Dropped out of four or five schools. Sang in hillbilly bars with a local bluegrass band. For the beer. "We'd do country songs, and then the band'd shut up and I'd sing blues, 'cause that was my thing."

Her thing was no Patti Page regatta, no Connie Francis sob-along, but mangy backwoods blues, heavy with devotion to Bessie Smith. She still smears Bessie across everything she sings, making it possible for a whole generation of us to hear beyond the scratches in those old records. But she says she never really tried to sing until she joined Big Brother.

"See, Bessie, she sang big open notes, in very simple phrasing. But you can't fall back on that in front of a rock band. I mean, you can't sing loose and easy with a throbbing amplifier and drums behind you. The beat just pushes you on. So I started singing rhythmically, and now I'm learning from Otis Redding to push a song instead of just sliding over it."

It was Chett Holmes who made Janis part of the Holding Company (before that, it had been an instrumental band, one of dozens formed during the merger of folk, jazz, and rock among Bay Area youth). From the start, their music began to clothe her voice. They taught her to blast, pound, and shatter a song. She returned the favor by directing her solos inward, toward the group's rhythmic heart. In fact, Janis has made her voice into a family.

It shows. People think of Big Brother and the Holding Company as more of a commune than a group.

True, it's chic to deride the band as being unworthy of her magic, but they are certainly not lame companions. Her voice is vast enough to overwhelm any accompaniment less raucous than a bazooka, but with Big Brother behind her, freaking out like country cousins, there is no difference between voice and music— just Sound. Call that the sound of Janis Joplin and you might as well identify a fire by its smoke just because that's what hits you first.

"I have three voices," she explains. "The shouter; the husky, gutteral chick; and the high wailer. When I turn into a nightclub singer, I'll probably use my husky voice. That's the one my mother likes. She says, 'Janis, why do you scream like that when you've got such a pretty voice?' "

It's not a pretty sound she makes now. A better word for it would be "primal." She plants herself onstage like a firmly rooted tree, then whips more emotion out of her upper branches than most singers can wring out of their lower depths. She slinks like tar, scowls like sunburn, stings like war. And she does one other thing that makes it all so sexy. She needs. Needs to move. Needs to feel. Needs to be screamed at. Needs to touch—and be touched back.

" 'Ball and Chain' is the hardest thing I do. I have to really get inside my head, everytime I sing it. Because it's about feeling things. That means I can never sing it without really trying. See, there's this big hole in the song that's mine, and I've got to fill it with something. So, I do! And it really tires me out. But it's so groovy when you know the audience really wants you. I mean, whatever you give them, they'll believe in. And they yell back at you, call your name, and—like that."

It's always the same: at Monterey, where the nation discovered her; at the Avalon, where they know her best; at the Anderson, where the New York press corps took notes; and tonight at the Electric Factory, in Philadelphia. She begs and coaxes her audiences until they begin to holler, first in cliches like "do-it-to-it" and finally in wordless squeals. Suddenly, the room is filled with the agony in her voice. Kids surround the stage, shouting her name and spilling over with the joy of having been reached. Even the onlookers in

neckties nod their heads and whisper "Shit . . . oh shit." Because to hear Janis sing "Ball and Chain" just once is to have been laid, lovingly and well.

Two sets later, they are back in the dressing room, flushed with sweat and applause. There is a tired hassle with the road manager. Dave the drummer changes into his third shirt that evening. And Janis is sitting on Gary the Gorilla's lap, fondling his furry knees and opening a second fifth of Southern Comfort.

"Why do I always hafta dance alone in these places?" she rasps, still recuperating from her solo. "I mean, you saw me dancing out there between sets. All those guys were standing around, panting in the corner. Finally, I had to say to one of 'em, 'Well, do you wanna dance, or not?' and he comes on waving his arms around like a fuckin' bat. Didn't even look at me. Now, why do things like that always happen?"

"Because you're so freaky looking," her road manager answers.

She nods slowly, and whispers, "Yeah."

She digs and detests her weirdness. She would like to be the freakiest chick in rock, and a gracious young lady as well. At a recent press party to celebrate the group's new contract with Columbia Records, Janis shook her hair only to confront a lady out of *Harper's Bazaar,* who covered up her drink and said, "Do you mind?" Janis answered in a tone out of *Evergreen,* "Fuck off, baby." But later she was seen pouting before a mirror, muttering, "Face it, baby, you've got ratty hair."

Now she moves out of the tiny room and surveys the remnants of this evening's scene: cigarette butts and a gaggle of local freaks. There are no pale young ladies searching for a seminal autograph in this crowd, but Peter the bassman is already making contact with a chick named Crafty. Gandalf, the wizard from the balcony, offers to read every palm in the house, whispering, "Hey—let's go up to your room and smoke."

Later, at a hamburger stand, Gandalf stops in the middle of a poem he is composing on a napkin and reflects: "Tomorrow, I'm gonna make it with Janis. I'm gonna just go up to her and say, 'Hey—let's make it.' 'Cause she's so groovy to watch. What a bod

she must have under that voice." He pauses to consider it, and then asks a waitress for spare whipped-cream cans.

But Gandalf the Wizard may have to wait longer than tomorrow. For this very night (while Philadelphia sleeps), Janis is with Gary the Gorilla, and they are finishing off the second fifth together.

—THE VILLAGE VOICE, 1968

# ● THE FAT ANGEL

The table in room 2227 at the St. Moritz is brimming. Dishes of butter and cream overflow in greasy spots. Strawberries and baked apples decay in the late afternoon sun. A mammoth salad drips with dressing. Broken rolls, empty Coke bottles, and a jug of fermenting apple cider frame an immense plate of clam shells. The lemon lies puckered to one side, drooped over an unopened bottle of Saccharin.

It's Cass Elliot's suite at 4 P.M. She sits behind the table among the formidable folds of a pink chiffon dressing gown, and smiles. "Good morning. I set the clock for 3:30, so I'd be up in time for you."

She is the real Cass—the fat one in the Mamas and the Papas. Hers is The Voice. The temptation is to compare it to a foghorn in tune, a humming tractor in third gear, or an eagle which has just sighted its dinner. But Cass is a screamer with a catch. Her voice floats somewhere between melody, harmony, and instrumentation. In "California Dreaming," she stretches notes like so much taffy. In "Monday, Monday," she is pure tenderizer.

If the Mamas and the Papas sing like a hurricane, Cass is the eye of the storm. John Phillips may write the group's gold records; Denny Doherty may croon melody; Michelle (John's wife) may supply the beauty; but Cass—a regal orange balloon in a flowing

59

muu-muu—hovers over all. She is the mother of the Mamas and the Papas.

She poses for pictures. ("Mind if I comb my hair?") She drapes across the couch to glance at the skyline which enters cautiously through her window. Her right hand, adorned with opals, moves as though to sign an autograph. But Cass picks up the phone and gingerly asks: "Would you send someone to pick up the tray? This is 2227 . . . thank you."

Cass is a superstar. Big enough to live in Natalie Wood's old house, a California palazzo with real grottos. Big enough to be on speaking terms with Brian Wilson, John Sebastian, and Ringo Starr. Big enough to feel like something is missing when she walks half a block without being stopped for an autograph.

Big enough to be Cass.

"I'm a teeny bopper in many respects. I'm overawed. The Beatles overawed me tremendously. When we were in England, I saw Ringo sitting in a bar, and I didn't even speak to him I was so amazed. 'Monday, Monday' was an enormous hit already, and he went back and told the rest of the Beatles that the Mamas and the Papas were snobs. But, I mean, what do you say: 'Hi, you don't know me but I'm Cass and you're Ringo?' "

Her adulation of the Beatles is thorough and exuberant. John Phillips told a concert audience recently: "Cass' aim in life is to rape John Lennon." To this charge Cass shakes her mighty brown curls in denial. But she admits that "bad press" about her devotion ("When I lived in Gramercy Park, I had a John Lennon collage that covered a whole wall—head shots, everything") resulted in a strained initial meeting between Cass and her idol.

Today, the Beatles dig the Mamas and the Papas. Who wouldn't? Theirs is the first thoroughly unique sound to hit the pop scene since the Beatles. Their two LPs have firmly established Cass and company as a top attraction. And their concert audiences are bigger and more demonstrative than ever.

Offstage, their act is painstakingly rehearsed and planned to the last dissonant note. Onstage, the Mamas and the Papas come on like four stoned kids having a groovy time singing. When Michelle cuts in on Cass' note, the two argue openly—which brings cheers of recognition from the audience. When police form a wedge to

prevent a last minute groupie-banzai, John blurts: "Whatdyamean we're busted?" Denny shuts his eyes tight during his solo, swaying back and forth as though he is floating on the notes.

And Cass . . . she bounds on the stage. She shakes her hand over the mike. She opens that perfect oval mouth and lets loose a round of perfect oval notes. She skirts harmonies around Denny's melodies. She gets introduced as "our orange mushroom." And between songs, she supplies an unending stream of patter: "I don't lose my voice, not at this price," or—the biggest laugh of the evening—"I've never done a boys' school before."

The Cass doll. Wind her up, she turns the world on. In exchange, everyone loves her. Fair exchange.

Cass the star. Lou Adler—a pioneer in surf, songs, car, and protest songs—gets the nod as her number-one angel. They call him "the fifth Mama." In a closely tailored beard and suit, he often accompanies the group to concerts. He stands in the wings listening to the sound, a tapered Bohemian; a mod with money.

Bio of Cass, the star-to-be, only recently laced with record sales figures and dollar signs. Naomi Cohen, born in Baltimore, 23 years ago. Raised in Washington, D.C. A bright child; a cute kid. Talked early, walked late. She remembers a driving intellect, a desire to do what there was to do.

Arrival of the star-to-be in New York: Cass lived in Greenwich Village, the Lower East Side, the Upper West Side—all the properly hip ghettos. The beatnik phase. Even then, there was the Cass image—the Cinemascope goddess.

"I don't have the psychology of the fat girl," she says. "I don't hide in corners. I'm a very verbose person. Everything I do is verbose."

Cass in a rainbow covered muu-muu, in sequins, in high socks and bull-whip-boots. She joined the Mugwumps, a legend after their time with John Sebastian and Zal Yanovsky. Then she teamed with Denny Doherty and Jim Hendricks in a super-polished hootenanny group called the Big Three in the days when folk was king. The Mugwumps never made it. The Big Three almost made it.

So Cass, who had studied acting in New York auditioned for the stage. That, too, didn't work. After one particularly disappointing tryout ("Abe Burrows wouldn't even look at me"), she went

home, piled her hanging hair under a gondolier's hat, draped her frame in a tapestry cape and made her way to 46th Street, to the theatre. When she reached the stage, she merely took off her hat, bowed deeply and walked out the door.

Here and now, Cass Elliot joins the widening ranks of teens and post-teens who made it as purveyors of the new style, children of the times—with ready bread. She has all the status pop music can bring a cheeky girl from Baltimore. Having finally cracked the great shell, she is too busy gobbling up what's inside to realize she is only eating peanut butter. She retains the Greenwich Village esprit, but she stops short of charging windmills. She compromises. This hurts, but not as much as anonymity.

"Compromising disturbs me," she says, "but not to the point where I'd rebel. Success changes your coloring. It's enabled me to do the things I've always wanted to do, and if I have to make compromises, well, that's part of being a celebrity."

Cass the celebrity doll. Her freaky friends run around the St. Moritz in fur vests and dungarees, spacing out the doormen. Donovan—who met her in L.A.—christens her the Fat Angel and writes a song of the same name.

Twilight mother. Lagoon queen. Strawberry sundae sibling. When you tell her: "To look at you is not everyday," she rears back her head and answers: "Maybe not for you, but for me it's everyday like this."

"What's your favorite food, Cass?"

"Cherrystone clams. I've been in New York four days, I've had nine dozen cherrystone clams."

"What do you think about miniskirts and long hair?"

"If the long hair covers the expanse from the miniskirt to the knees, its okay. Miniskirts are very dangerous. My mother's always telling me not to bend over."

"What should teenagers do about their parents?"

"Be very patient."

"What do you think of Murray The K?"

"How can anybody be a rock 'n' roll disc jockey and wear Sam Snead hats?"

"Phil Spector?"

"I love Spector."

"Why?"

"I think he's a hobbit."

Now that she has finally won the pop music derby, Cass is anxious to run another race on a different track. She wants to make a movie, "not a Mamas-and-the-Papas-Go-to-the-Moon kind of thing, but a serious film. Ideally, we'd want Theodore Sturgeon to write it, and Orson Welles to direct."

She wants to get out of California because "it's a police state. I know, because I bought an Aston-Martin and I put a Reagan sticker on it, only because I know if I'm speeding through Orange County late at night with a Reagan sticker on that kind of expensive car, I'll never be stopped. If I were in a Renault, I might go to jail."

She wants to be the new pop-art girl; she isn't so sure pop-art wants her. "All the other Warhol girls are so silent," she says. "If there's one thing I'm not, it's silent. Even when I'm standing still, I'm not silent."

Cass sat for two Andy Warhol screen tests, which she calls a "Zen experience. He didn't even talk to me. He sent someone over to tell me to sit in a chair and not smile or be affected by anything. It totally spaced me out."

The spacing out was mutual. Warhol's suggestion was a 70-minute movie entitled *The New Beauty*—in which Cass would be surrounded by beautiful boys. Cass demurred because "it was an image I wouldn't want to project, the mother figure. I'm just not camp."

The clown doll; fond of antiques, old Vernon Duke songs, *The Rise and Fall of the City of Mahogany*. Kooky, kicky Cass. Her groovy fab-gear existence. Hovering around 200 pounds. Resplendent in rouge and greasepaint and a generously cut tent dress. Wind her up, she makes you laugh.

But Cass is much more than a fat Mama. She is a new kind of goddess. There is a helping of Mae West and just a pinch of Clyde Beatty. But beyond camp, Cass is Cass. She has broken the strongest barrier for an aspiring star. In America, the most weight-conscious nation in the world, she has become a glamour girl. She is a star, not despite her weight or because of it, but beyond it. Cass is a horizon.

"How do you feel about your weight?"

"I don't know."

"Well, do you feel any different from the way you've ever felt?"

"I've always been fat. Except when I was four, maybe."

"Has it become a commodity?"

"No. Getting clothes used to be a problem. Now I have everything made."

"Does anyone ever advise you to lose weight?"

"Only my closest friends."

"And your business associates?"

"They'd be terrified."

There aren't many subjects Cass is reluctant to talk about. Ask about psychedelic music and she shoots off her mouth, while her press agent blanches. "I resent everyone cashing in on consciousness expansion. It's a personal thing that doesn't belong to the man on the street who doesn't do it. LSD may have changed the face of rock 'n' roll, but I've never heard any psychedelic music—except maybe Scheherazade—that paints pictures for me."

On Vietnam she prefers to remain silent, but insists: "If we expressed ourselves on Vietnam," she says of the group, "it wouldn't be what the elders wanted us to say."

But on the subject of diet, Cass clams up. Her answers are evasive; her terse wit is vague; her anecdotes become generalities. She once weighed 300 pounds; she lost 70, gained 30 back. On a hospital starvation diet, she developed gout after eight days and was released. "I want to do something right away or not at all," she admits.

"Why are you fat, Cass?"

An inscrutable silence.

"I don't know. . . . Everyone has fears, I guess. In my mind, I've thought that my weight protects me. See, I'm a very gullible person. If you tell me anything seriously, I'll believe you. An attractive young girl in this world who is gullible can get herself into a lot of trouble and I find that . . . it keeps the lechers away. Whatever psychological reason motivates me to stay heavy also motivates me to succeed . . . eventually, I'll lose it all."

Cass the superstar. The camp creature. The California Dreamer. To those bits, add one more: Cass the pro.

The Mamas and the Papas are one of the most musically literate

groups on the pop scene; their versatility is due in no small measure to the Cass Elliot sound. But Cass is an entertainer beyond the mechanics of her music. She knows how to twist and lift her audience with a smile here, a shimmy there. And offstage, she is all there—really there. Behind the greasepaint and the echo chambers, she is a professional Cass.

You can never know for sure about these things, but when Cass Elliot says she enjoys her money and her fame, you feel like believing her. There is nowhere she would rather be than where she's at.

"I'm doing what I want and I'm being accepted," she declares. "When people who get respect respect you, that's the most important thing. I'm not afraid of being left behind by anything— short of bubble dancing. I just sing and enjoy it and let everyone watch me."

Donovan says Cass is the Fat Angel. He might as well have called her Tinkerbelle, sprinkling magic dust over a grooving generation. She teaches her listeners how to listen. They love her for it. They buy her records.

To which Cass Elliot just winks, gobbles a dozen cherrystone clams, and sings.

—NEW YORK MAGAZINE, 1967

# ● HARLEQUIN IN NEON

Flight 711 coasts into Las Vegas at twilight, when the desert sky is flected with color-dust. Neon sparkles everywhere. Whole streets move at stroboscopic speed. Buildings blink and twirl like colossal blossoms of light. The very air seems charged with a dry electric musk.

Vegas is the fake-crystal chandelier in the American pleasure dome. And the biggest bauble of all is Caesar's Palace, a hotel devoted to the principle that vulgarity in excess is what magnificence is all about. As the taxi glides past its arcade (one hundred fifty feet of floodlighted fountains in a garden of pseudoclassic statuary) my eyes are assaulted by a Cinerama billboard, which proclaims its message in letters seven feet high: TINY TIM.

America's current curio-in-residence, a Quasimodo to the middle classes, is appearing twice nightly in the Circus Maximus Room, amid the jangle of rhinestones and currency. Harlequin in neon; he's right up there, immortalized beside the topless earth-mother-a-go-go. Local newspapers are filled with planted items about his eccentricities. You can't avoid his iridescent falsetto on the radio. Souvenir stands hawk "rickie-tickie-stickie" decals with his name embossed. And tourists brandish plastic tulips in his honor.

But, even if his hype-squad hadn't showered Vegas with a promo-

tion budget ample enough to feed a ghetto, Tiny Tim would have overwhelmed this town on his own. Nothing can stop a freak whose time has come. And this is Tiny's moment. With death and damnation cluttering our front parlors (not to mention our bedrooms), what would be a safer phenomenon than this celery stalk with soul. Johnny Carson can count on a knowing snicker from his audience when he mutters "Tiny Tim kills bugs dead." (Get it? Flit!) Now, when crowds tire of punch lines about ungrateful kids and spiteful mothers-in-law, there is always Tiny Tim. "Have you heard, he's entering the Miss America pageant?" goes a typical routine. "He's representing Death Valley."

Tiny himself is less than delighted with his role as show-biz scapegoat. Under the veil of cosmetic camp, he sees himself as a wandering minstrel. His aim may be nostalgic, but his immediate effect is comic. Tiny is not the first troubadour to survive by playing the clown. But his successes have been so interlaced with ridicule, that he has come to value mockery the way most performers dig applause.

"This clown role is something I've always lived with," he admits. "In the old days, they didn't want legitimate singing from me. I was hired strictly as a novelty. But nothing mattered more to me than selling my songs. Even today, that's true. If they think of me as a harlequin, that doesn't bother me, as long as they appreciate what I sing."

Ah, but they love it. At the slot machines, they chant his name like a mantra. In a supersnack bar called the "Noshorium," a spangle-ridden lady clutches tulips to her breast and warbles "Let's see Tiny Tim. He's my favorite freak." Beautiful people adore him for his chic; ugly people find him more enchanting than the Three Stooges. The underground worships his saintly cool, while the overground is dazzled by his market potential. Kids shine in his presence, as though he were a prince out of Hans Christian Andersen. And bevies of boppers are dying to be the first in their tract developments to make Tiny Tim.

But I could never stomach him. Before his canonization by Johnny Carson I used to watch him warm up crowds at the Scene, a rock cellar off Times Square. He'd stand there, his cheeks aglow

in the discoglare. The floor around him was alive with buttocks (because in Times Square, they dance with only their hips). In some damp and darkened corner, I would always spot some chick cracking up over his makeup. Of course, I hadn't known him as Larry Love or Derry Dover, I'd never seen him play a freak show on Eighth Avenue or a tourist trap in the Village. I hadn't even caught him singing on the subways, when there was no other gig to be had. He was just another disassembled gnome to me, and watching him perform, I couldn't shake the impression that he was laying bare the folds of his soul to ridicule and anticipating the result. That scene frightened me, always has.

No wonder I am still uptight about Tiny Tim. Three years and superstardom have done little to change his act or diminish my fear. So I proceed with caution toward the Atrium Room, where Tiny is holding a reception for his "dear friends" among the press. Ahead of me, a burly local with a string tie bisecting his Adam's apple, shouts, "Thar he is. By gosh, I thought he was colored."

Inside, I spot Tiny right away, leaning against a panel of marbleized wallpaper, in a baggy black raincoat. It distinguishes him from his retinue of tailored hairlines and suppressed wastes. These promo men take turns squiring Tiny around the floor. The whole ritual is danced like a pallid minuet. Tiny curtsies with his wrist and performs a short, sprinting twirl. But his smile is frozen in place and in his eyes, I notice a deep tinge of exhaustion.

So that's how they do it. Shove him through the crowd like a greased ax cutting oak. Dangle those universal carrots of love and mass acclaim before his eyes. And when he begins to look a little soggy, lift his spirit with a shot of that universal elixir—cold cash.

The underground press has been full of stories about Tiny Tim being mesmerized by his managers. But I've never been able to buy that myth. A man is victimized by his own desire, and then finds surrogate figures to shoulder the blame. I offer in evidence, Richard Perry, the twenty-six-year-old producer who has masterminded Tiny's current success. Perry first met his client in 1965, when Tiny was going the door-to-door route to obsolescence. "I took one look at him and classified him as another Tin Pan Alley freak," Perry explains. "But then he started to sing—you know, standing there with his ukulele. And my mind was shattered. I took

him back to my office and just sat there for hours recording him."

Perry has seen Tiny come a long way since then. Every inch the proud guardian, he watches Tiny out of the corner of his drink while I question him about the show. It is going over well, though its star is still nervous about all those dancing girls.

"He looks a little . . . uncomfortable," I prod. Perry stares into the fizzy depths of his drink. "Well," he whispers, "he's still getting adjusted to his new environment."

1958 was a smug, clean-shaven year in anyone's book. But for Herberto Buckingham Kaury, it must have been hell in small doses. He moved through the streets of Upper Manhattan with his makeup and his shopping bag. The kids called him "Crazy Herbie" and celebrated his every appearance with a hail of abuse. With his dish-rag hair and his face like a demolished Edsel, he was ugly as sin. And in 1958, ugly WAS sin.

But he resisted (out of psychic need, if not pride) and his protest took the form of protective fantasy. He built a sturdy wall of nostalgia around his mind, filtering all external experience through a rosy haze of recollections. The raw material of his collage came from those classic havens for the tormented: movies and music. Others may have looked upon him as an outcast, but he saw himself as a wind chime, held against the breeze of memory.

"I used to close the door to hear my records," he recalls. "I had to be alone, in the dark, because then I could feel I was in the phonograph with the singers, feeling their voices inside me. And it was the same with movies. I always went alone. I'd see six movies a day—from twelve noon till twelve at night. Films about the 1890's or early 1900's I'd run to. There seems to be a yearning in my heart for that period. I'd like to live each of those days in good health. Everything was so . . . meticulous then."

Within the strict confines his psyche imposed, "Crazy Herbie" was creating a fantasy cosmos for himself, rich with poignant emotion. It is that vision—not its accoutrements—which makes him a celebrity today. One generation's outcast is another's superstar.

No one calls him "Crazy Herbie" anymore. He lives in ornamental splendor now, brushing up against the haut monde, and signing autographs for the maid. His suite at Caesar's Palace is

brimming over with gold leaf and crushed velvet. And from the window of his living room, you can see that billboard with just the words T I N Y peering over the horizon.

He rises late, to a breakfast of honey and sunflower seeds. This is the basis of his celebrated diet—although he wavers from it in expansive moods. On his first night in Vegas, he ordered everything on the room-service menu. The bill came to $185, and when the food arrived, Tiny arranged it all over his suite and then just sat in the middle of it. Word raced through the hotel that he had actually rolled in it, but this, he emphatically denies. "I saw it in an Edward Arnold movie," he explains.

I arrive at his suite at 4 P.M. Tiny's road manager—Ron De Blasio—ushers me into a plush chair and fetches me a Diet-Rite. De Blasio is largely responsible for the "class" in Tiny's act. For Vegas audiences, that means gauzy drapes, dry-ice fog and pirouetting chorines in togas. (They call it "the Botticelli number.") There are no Tiny Tim dolls on the market yet. But De Blasio admits he was tempted by an offer from a ukulele company. "We turned it down," he explains, "because we figured that in six weeks, every kid in the country would have one. Then Tiny would get known as a novelty."

That seems to be the strategy behind this promotion campaign. They are selling Tiny like a Presidential candidate who must last awhile. After all, his talent runs deeper than his drag. The voices he sings in range from booming baritone to vivid vibrato. His practiced ear can absorb almost any vocal style, and his current act includes some flawless blasts from the distant past (Rudee Vallee, Russ Columbo, Cab Callaway, and even Elvis Presley). The men who manage him (Campbell, Silver, and Cosby, Inc.) are letting the public experience Tiny an octave at a time.

"Hell—o, Mr. Goldstein." Tiny greets me with ten bouquets of daffodils in his voice. But I remain suspicious. Deep down, I want to discover the *real* (i.e., decadent) Tiny Tim. I want to write about the plastic cruelty of his public, or the poison suckle of his managers.

But my slant has already been undermined by his fans—especially the kids. They sneak up to the front desk and ask to speak with Tiny on the house phone. They run down the corridors

giggling at the mention of his name. Occasionally, they knock on my door, convinced that anyone with long hair is a distant cousin possessing some contagious magic. Their joy blows my cool. What do they see that the rest of us miss? I ask a transfixed four-year-old why Tiny Tim is so special. "Because he's all cute," she stammers, then runs off giggling.

Tiny himself is mystified by the marshmallow glee he inspires. He is confident that children will tire of him, as they did of Soupy Sales. But his appeal among the very young may be more durable than he thinks. He has never cultivated kids, yet they seek him out at every concert. In fact, Tiny Tim is the only recent children's celebrity to emerge without benefit of regular exposure on daytime television.

He has earned their allegiance by simply being himself. To understand why, it's necessary to consider what a clown accomplishes when he does his thing. Because children experience clowns differently than the rest of us do. They know instinctively that slapstick is a ruse, to disarm an audience. Once we are in that state, a good clown can move us with the mere suggestion of emotion in his walk—or even his props. Great clowns balance fear, pity, mischief, and ridicule on the tips of their noses.

And the truly immortal clown—a harlequin for the ages—balances the most slippery emotion of all: innocence. He can make us feel holy by putting us in the company of one who has never sinned. If Charlie Chaplin had come of age in Greenwich Village he might have called himself Tiny Tim.

Far from the ebb and flow of coin into machine, Tiny slips a pair of earphones over his antelope's head and smears his neck with Vick's Vaporub. Warms the throat.

"This one is short and sweet," booms the control room.

"Yes, Mr. Perry." Everyone is Mister to Tiny. If he doesn't know your last name he is liable to call you something like Mister Richard.

"Take a look at those words." Tiny picks up the envelope at his side and studies the lyrics he's supposed to cut today. It's "Hello, Hello," the old Sopwith Camel hit, filled with conscious innocence. Maybe a little too conscious for Tiny. He says, "It needs more words, it's too new. Can I change it around?"

De Blasio rushes in. "It's so you, Tiny.... It fits you like a suit.... Don't you see? ... This makes great SENSE to sing."

That last phrase hits Tiny right between the eyes. When they mess with his music, Tiny starts to growl ("UMMMFFFF") and if they persist, he breaks into an intolerable whine. But words like "sense" are powerful tranquilizers, and they can be dangled above his head like a pacifier.

The song is cut in twenty takes. Tiny's voice is nearly gone, and his throat reeks of Vicks. But when the session breaks, he finds a piano at the back of the studio and begins to play. "A hit can be made in the bathtub," he observes as I pull up an extra chair. "You don't need these big studios. But everything's so technical today."

We talk about his music. He throws a dozen names at me from the antique charm bracelet in his mind. Names like Henry Burr and Billy Murray, Irving Kauffman, Anita Jones. "I'd like to use more of their authentic sounds in my music. I want to try singing through a megaphone to give people a sense of what actually went on."

Then he begins to play a song I've never heard before. Its melody is pure music box, and his voice is the toy ballerina spinning on top.

> If I could drive a spaceship
> I'd take you to the stars
> And you would be alone with me
> As we fly next to Venus and Mars ...*

As he sings, I feel a smile spreading across my face, like sunrise. His voice is so gentle, so powerful, and so sad. Tiny looks up, and I can see him blush.

De Blasio rushes in from the control booth. "We'll put it in the show tonight. It's beautiful, Tiny. Doncha see? It's about this guy who would do anything for his chick—even go to the moon. But he just hasn't got the stuff. He's so beautiful, though, because he's up there on the moon already, so he doesn't care."

Tiny winces and begins to grunt. "I don't do my own numbers in public," he says flatly. "Because these songs are written especially for girls. I wrote that for Miss Snookie, at the Page Three."

De Blasio studies the perforations in the soundproof ceiling. "But Tiny," he whispers, "that just doesn't make sense."

* Copyright © 1968, Tiny Tim.

For two years Tiny sang at the Page Three, a Greenwich Village club "where the ladies liked each other." He insists that engagement was more meaningful than his current supergig at Caesar's Palace. And he means it. In 1963, that cellar was the nexus of his existence —the one place where his outer and inner worlds met and made music together.

When he came on, all fidgeting ceased, and the ladies settled back into their seats. Then the lights went up on this scrawny mantis plucking a uke and bouncing on the balls of his feet. And then he sang:

> If you ever said good-bye
> I'd feel depressed and yet
> I'd never cry
> For you would always be
> In every memory
> You are heaven here on
> earth to me.

After his act was over, they stomped and shrieked for more. And the gargoyle onstage—who went to all of their parties and spent his spare bread cutting records for the ladies he loved—would blow these whispy puffs of gratitude from his lips.

What moved them then—and still does—is an aura of innocence so potent that it transcends Tiny's surroundings and makes him holy. I ask him to define *purity,* and he surprises me by answering with the ease of a man who is aware of his effect on others. "It's a spiritual fulfillment which comes with obeying God's laws."

The agnostic in me bristles. I draw angry boxes around his words on my pad. "Which are God's laws?"

"Well, the first test is with women. We're not supposed to touch women until marriage. That means, no kissing or contact—except for talking."

"But what if your body tells you it's right to kiss a woman?"

"There are devil's angels and heaven's angels. A devil's angel will say it's perfectly permissible. But then, he couldn't be an angel from heaven because that kind of angel would follow heaven's laws."

This begins to sound like a scene from *Quo Vadis,* I feel like a Roman profligate facing a martyr in the making. "What happens if you disobey these laws?" I ask.

His voice drops to a firm baritone. "Ah—you suffer."

Still, it would be a mistake to label Tiny Tim a puritan. He is too
tolerant of sin in others and would probably make a lousy inquisitor.
("People's scenes don't bother me," he explains, "because I'm not
after anything.") His world-view reminds me of a tapestry in Vic-
torian needlepoint. All the figures are neatly etched in place, and
the border is decorated with faded magenta blossoms. Yet, the whole
canvas seems static, as though the notion of true sin were too fluid
for him to capture in cloth.

His managers are aware of even this chink in Tiny's psychic
armor, and don't think they aren't prepared to exploit it. Says De
Blasio: "I've often thought, looking at that profile, that some day
I'd like Tiny to do a record of Bible readings."

"Even when I was younger, my father said I looked like Jesus,"
he admits.

"How did it feel being told that?"

"Very tempestuous. It frightened me to look like Christ."

Tiny is the product of a mixed marriage (father, Jewish; mother,
Catholic). That he favors his dear mother should be no surprise,
since his entire cosmology is centered around women. He shuns all
male toiletries and keeps a generous supply of cosmetic creams.
("This new cream—I ordered 150 jars—it makes your face look
just like a julep.") Yet, those who are consoled by the notion that
Tiny is a transvestite (or at least, gay) are in for a rude shock. He is
as straight as a yardstick and just as flexible. He is convinced that
S-E-X (he won't even utter the word, or any other "swear," except
for a plaintive "sh—ucks") is evil unless sanctified by marriage,
and he can't get married unless he sees a sign from heaven.

"Maybe in the next world, I'll have all the women I want," he
muses "but not in this one."

"Tiny . . ." I stammer. "Do you . . . want to sleep with women?"

"Yesss." He nearly falls off his seat with eagerness. "I don't want
to behave this way. But it's one of God's supreme laws, you see. It's
like going against a red light. Oh, it's so hard sometimes. I try
never to be alone with a beautiful woman. Because, when I'm
alone, the devil in me becomes dangerous."

"What happens then?" I ask, trying to look casual.

"Well . . ." he slides into his deepest voice yet. "I have fallen a

few times." I blink and take a hefty swig of Diet-Rite. "But if I do something wrong with a girl, I can't see her again unless it's like nothing ever happened. I've got to cut the cancer out and start anew."

I am unprepared to deal with Tiny Tim as a functioning (i.e., competing) male, so I begin to nibble on the end of my pen, a sure sign I have lost control of the interview.

"I got involved with someone in 1966," he continues. "I had never gone with a woman before, but I said yes to her. I found out I'm no good to be tied down. She tried to have me stop my cosmetics . . . there was bickering night and day."

"Why do you wear makeup?"

"Oh, when I put on my face, I feel that I'm in a garden of paradise alone with beautiful ladies. They are the essence of my soul . . . a purity that cannot be tainted."

Tiny's manager (who has been sitting between us) announces that dinner has arived. A beaming waiter wheels in eight goblets of sherbert and two huge malteds. For the voice. I make notions to leave, but first I ask Tiny what he would do if he ever met his soul lady for real. He stops and gazes out at the gold-lamé sunset in the distance, "I'll do anything to get her into my web," he says. "I've got to know her . . . to keep her. If nothing else works . . . I'll get to her boyfriend."

With fifteen minutes till showtime we sit in Tiny's dressing room talking about Johnny Carson ("I feel nothing but gratitude toward him,") and Bob Dylan ("He believed in me from the very start") and John Lennon. ("He was supposed to introduce me at the Albert Hall, but now I believe it's going to be Prince Philip. Can you imagine what Princess Margaret's face creams must be like?")

For once, I'm not afraid to laugh at his lines. I understand his hang-ups and appreciate the power of his modesty. But I have to confront him with a final myth: the one which claims that Tiny has been poisoned. He doesn't look moribund to me, but there are persistent reports of orgies and all-night drunks. His manager did have to move in with him at one point, and De Blasio still shares his quarters occasionally. So I pop the question, fully expecting a sanctimonious denial. Instead, he replies for real.

"When I first came to Hollywood, there were lots of temptations.

It was so new, so strange . . . like going to the top of a mountain that so many try to climb. After you get there, you linger awhile and rest. I did have a drink here and there, though I didn't like the bitter taste. You know, back in May, I was alone in a hotel room. So, I had a few. And I had a few people over. And I spent some money. I was dizzy . . . I've been that way before."

Maybe what the underground can't accept is Tiny's willing embrace of success. Show business is such a squid, why would anyone hustle it willingly? But Herberto Buckingham Kaury has always wanted to make it big, and that has always meant Las Vegas, and candy fog and dancing girls. He would even sacrifice his innocence if it made SENSE. He is aware of alternatives, and strong enough to choose. His choice for now is that it is better to burn in neon than to freeze in the dark. Tiny remembers the dark well. He used to deliver people's teeth in it, when that was the only work he could get.

"I fought for this challenge all along," he says. "It's like a ball game for me. Every show is another inning."

So I leave him with his manager and climb a long flight of stairs until I can see the entire backstage of that velvet veldt they call the Circus Maximus. Vestal virgins grab a smoke in the wings . . . amid the tangle of cardboard columns, orchestral clatter fills the air. Tiny Tim is also warming up. I see him in a corner, trotting in place and flaying the air with his hands. Then he goes into his windup: right hand back, left foot out, and there's the pitch—a wicked spitball curve. And he watches, delighted, as the batter in his head strikes out.

OK, Tiny. Play it your way. I don't mind anymore. In fact, there's something to be said for a guy who understands his true role in life and makes it matter.

—EYE, 1968

# ● BREAKING BREAD WITH THE WIZARD OF OZ

"Art is anything you can get away with."
—MARSHALL MCLUHAN

"Humbledey, hubledy, humbley, bumbdley, fum (thank you)."
—JOHN LENNON


He stands complacent against a skyline of microphones, face robust with the suntan of television makeup. The rest of us—reporters and personnel—sit to one side, pencils raised like antennae. We have already signed pieces of paper giving CBS permission to film us observing the event. Now, as the camera rolls, A and R man John Simon signals Columbia Records' latest discovery, and it is "take" whatever, for the press.

Since early morning, Marshall McLuhan has been filling tracks of tape with a barrage of anti-concepts from *The Medium Is the Massage,* the teleological coloring book which now tops the best-seller list for paperbacks. This is the metamorphosis of an oracle into a recording star, and if Studio B is not exactly Delphi, the current oracle needs no temple, just lots of electricity. His is the immortality of the moment, which is just as profound as timelessness.

McLuhan is a soft-sell declaimer. He pauses triumphantly after every phase like Orson Welles with a hard-on: "All media work us

over completely. They are so pervasive in their personal, political, economic, aesthetic, psychological, moral, ethical, and social consequences that they leave no part of us untouched, unaffected, unaltered. The medium is the massage."

Well, okay, I think we've got the rub. He is the Wizard of Oz, and we are all Dorothys from flat, clean Kansas, uprooted by the electric cyclone and thrust into emerald cities with button-down priests, instant ritual, and a napalm liturgy. So we ask the Wizard, "What's it all about?" That stern, sandpaper voice pulses with cryptic half-revelation: "Two fried eggs and a cup of Indonesia." "We shape our tools and thereafter our tools ape us." "Schizophrenia may be a necessary consequence of literacy."

Ask a simple question and the Wizard answers with a left jab to the ego. You find yourself boxing with his books and wrestling with his wordgames, but Marshall McLuhan's ambiguity is an essential part of his magic. After all, it is not his ideas but his cryptic cool that sets him apart from the academicians. We could tolerate a man who disputes the time-honored "content" principle. We could even accept a man who implies that the Renaissance and the Dark Ages were one and the same. Modern thought treasures its enfants terribles. But McLuhan crosses the style barrier which separates iconoclasts from mischief makers. He wears the royal purple of a celebrity over his dark scholar's suit. He is our first para-philosopher, as concerned with the sound of a concept as with its meaning. "Insistence on hard-headed clarity issues from a sentimental feeling," his recorded voice conjectures. "Insistence on clarity at all costs is based on sheer superstition as to the mode in which human intelligence functions."

McLuhan's response to the compartmentalization of modern education is to label it a product of the printing press. His logic is in celebration of spontaneous perception. He is not so much a student of media as its first unrepentant poet. He has built a cosmology on a series of concept-barbs; they catch and take hold. His theories spread in whirlpools. There is no logical progression, no Hegelian synthesis, but an instant, almost pentecostal revelation. The moment is urgent for McLuhan. His eyes shine and his grin expands at the very contemplation of a word ruse. His books are filled with puns, puzzles, and linguistic punching bags. Even when

his ideas sink into a mire, his words are buoyant; they sound as though they belong. It is probably subversive to consider McLuhan's Media Verse his most valuable contribution, but that joyous verbosity is really what keeps us marveling and reading on.

Marshall McLuhan is the James Joyce of Madison Avenue. His well-publicized contempt for academic thought stems from its proximity. Before he was the Wizard of Oz, McLuhan was a Joycean scholar. Phrases from *Finnegan's Wake* still dot his speech. "The earth it orbs," he observes. "It's a form that has become planetary. Mumford doesn't realize that yet." We reporters munch our three-cornered sandwiches and nod. The emerald city plies its wizards with laurel wreaths and cold cash (a best seller, a TV special, a pampered position at a major university). The people of Oz don't demand that their wizards be right, only magic. If there is melancholia behind McLuhan's ascendancy it is probably that the burden of being perpetually profound makes all magicians inhuman.

Uptight in basic business black, McLuhan sips a gin and tonic and exults over Twiggy. She is enigmatic; her presence cries out for explanation, and McLuhan (who knows that wizards are logicians of the absurd) makes an inspired guess. "Twiggy is geometric . . . She represents a turn away from the pictorial . . ." and finally, the abracadabra metaphor:

"Only Euclid
Has looked on
Twiggy bare."

He even parries questions like a poet, reshaping them into a reply that is potent on its own terms. "Why do boys wear long hair?" a hangdog lady asks, her lips jutting forward in attentive folds:

"They want involvement
IN volvement
Their hair envelopes them
Like a placenta."

Her lips button shut. "I can't read your books more than two pages at a sitting. I get lost."

The Wizard pauses for a sip and a stare. "Try speedreading," he advises and then launches into a cosmic discourse about linear scan

and literacy, finally concluding that "Milton is a natural for speed-reading. He's all pictures."

McLuhan's put-downs are extraterritorial. They begin with the subject at hand, but soon wander into free verse. There is arrogance for those who call him a huckster, impatience for those who do not understand, and a baffled disapproval for some of those who think they do. "People like to be taken in," he says. "They think it's safe."

Outside the Columbia Recording studio, and a few blocks east, dozens of ad-men are walking around like platonic princes since the McLuhan magic hit town. TV executives have been observed glowing with pride at the possibility that standards are irrelevant. Even hippies are enticed. There are tribes of McLuhanistic poets and artists. House organs like the *Oracle* sing his praises in elvish. He has become a synonym for anything that is inexplicable, and hippies see a lot of territory yet to be charted.

McLuhan himself is miffed by hip indulgence. "Kids are loaded with expectations for the cool millennium," he says. "I don't know where these people get the idea that I approve of these developments. I don't think evolution is necessarily a desirable thing. I find it vile."

He doesn't like the underground. He only chronicles it. "Happenings shouldn't happen to a dog," he snaps. "These are despicable, revolting people," he says of hippies. "Los Angeles is not McLuhan country," he contradicts, delighted that people are calling it that.

The conflict between the man and his message is unmistakable. For all his exaltation in print about involvement, McLuhan is aloof and suspicious in person; *wizards are distant.* For all his comprehension of the electronic eye he will always be a dot-and-dash man. He sounds stiff on record and looks uncomfortable on TV; *wizards are themselves the victims of media.* He had made heroes of advertisers and prophets of hippies and yet he says he hates them both. He claims to have "no illusions about the ability of academic men to perceive anything," and yet he has accepted a $100,000 position at Fordham University; *wizards are paradoxical.* He claims: "I have no theories, only probes," and yet he has been known to shuck philosophic systems like a TV viewer changing channels. He refracts impressions like a prism; *wizards are cryptic.*

You can watch Marshall McLuhan without ever seeing him. You can eat with the Wizard of Oz without ever breaking bread with him. The stage make-up never cracks. His cool demands the kind of self-distance that obscures rapport; *wizards are contained.*

He delights in word-gags, double entendres, and linguistic slapstick. At lunch with a literary crowd, he interrupts a discourse about Vietnam to define a gynecologist as "a spinner of old wives' tails." He caps a discussion on the significance of the guitar in modern culture by muttering: "It's a bad cold," letting his company squirm a little before he reveals that it was not "guitar" but "catarrh" that he was thinking of.

McLuhan's gospel is filled with old gags in search of a punchline. In fact, his best work distorts cliches for dramatic effect, as in a dialectical theatre of the absurd. A young girl's voice on the record asks, "Why did the moron take a ladder to church?" while an audience laughs and an elevator bell rings. A voice replies: "Oh God, I'm hungry." Later on, after McLuhan ad-libs a joke about a Boy Scout who helps a nun across the street and assures her that "Any relative of Batman is a friend of mine," the girl asks: "Do you like your job, Professor McLuhan?"

Professor McLuhan never answers that question, and not many people will insist on a reply. We assume our wizards are happy because they are influential. This one looks happy; he bristles with certainty. And he warns the press: "We're going to pour things over on this archaic village called New York."

But this city is a medium with its own massage. Men who define the moment carry stopwatches. The Wizard of Oz must know that fame itself is tactile. In between puns and revelations, he steps behind his silver screen and declares: "The best jokes are grievances."

Marshall McLuhan kids around a lot.

—THE VILLAGE VOICE, 1967

# ● RAVI AND THE
# TEENIE SATORI

They are waiting for him in the glass-enclosed library of Asia House, over coffee, cream, and croissants. All the regulars are there; the lady reporter in her tweed uniform nibbles gingerly on a breakfast bun. A tall angular gentleman is delivering his pre-recorded monologue about last summer's visit to Madras. Two Indians in mercantile mufti are warbling metaphysics: "One must live alone to survive in the modern world," one chortles to the other. And a day-glo journalist, lean and oozing television, stops a hostess in swirling sari and demands: "Spell that—will ya?" She answers with a wisp-lisp caress in her voice: "S-i-t-a-r."

Then he walks in, hands neatly folded like two starched handkerchiefs under his chin, beige-muslin tunic over creased black pants, hair in neat curls over his collar. He smiles the sweet smile of saintly patience, the immaculate presence of an artist.

In the corner of the room, two reporters from *Datebook* magazine are fiddling with a Brownie camera and a tape recorder. Having bandied about questions of etiquette (how do you address an Indian superstar?), they nudge each other between the lady reporter and the ersatz Britisher. With glitter in their eyes, and clucking bopper noises on their lips, they approach the master to ask their timid question.

"Whatdya think of George?"

TV-face butts in with a 21-inch grin and a handshake in living

color. "Mr. Shankar, I'm pleased to meet ya." The sweet face smiles back in non-recognition. To his right, the Anglophile is recounting autumn in Darjeeling; to his left the tweed lady is discussing the feasibility of a mini-sari. But *Datebook*'s microphone is hovering about his teacup, so he answers into it: "I have accepted George as my disciple. He is not at all like other pop musicians. But I have nothing to do with him as a Beatle."

The girls from *Datebook* smile thank you before they are pushed away by an Asia House question about the evolution of the tabla in the "raga sound." Back in their corner, one of them observes: "He's got such soft hands to shake." And a high-school girl, doing a term paper on the sitar, answers: "He's a lot cuter than Ali (Akbar Khan)."

He is Ravi Shankar, master of the sitar and India's crown jewel in the coffers of world music. He is in New York to give three concerts at Philharmonic Hall, and to accept a citation for "distinguished achievement in creating and advancing American interest in Indian music and culture."

At 46, he has watched and heard and touched the Western world as no Eastern musician before him. He wrote those piercing death-screams into Satyajit Ray's film trilogy. In London, he recently completed the music for a British TV production of "Alice in Wonderland." His American audience, strong and long-faithful to the master, is centered in cities and college towns—where it counts.

And so Ravi Shankar wears the look of a man who has patiently endured all the praise-without-comprehension an alien culture can bestow. He has been Martian-in-residence for years. He smiles and observes: "It gives me great pleasure to see people without any background in our music appreciating it." But he objects to ads like the one placed by a record company in his concert program, advising the curious to take a peek at the primitive folk sounds of India. ("After all," soothes the copy, "a little Eastern exposure never hurts anyone.") "I do not play folk or primitive songs," he declares. "This is classical music."

Ravi Shankar stands untouched amid all that grasping splendor. He neither accepts nor rejects the adulation but he watches it all with ice-and-fire eyes. He wears the expression of a man who has

been complimented many times for speaking English well, even though it is his nation's official language. He reaches out for a cookie, a handshake, or a question with a subtle sobriety that makes his audience feel like the foreigner. And he treats reporters with the same sense of equality a farmer shows all of his livestock.

Ravi Shankar's "new" audience responds with all the garlands it usually bestows on its idols, but without the frenzy. After all, he isn't shouting rape-with-a-beat to an audience of truncated virgins. He doesn't even play rock 'n' roll. He merely influences, stealthily, cryptically. He encourages by merely tolerating. So much of folk-rock is a superficial offshoot of his work that he evokes from the teeniebopper legions a quality they seldom display to their idols: unadorned respect.

During his concerts, the audience brims with sought-after satori. On an Indian carpet, surrounded with wafting incense, he makes love to this weird giraffe of an instrument they call a sitar. He strokes and pets it; makes it groan and whine; he tickles its belly and rubs its back. His bare feet, knotted at rest, keep the beat.

When the concert ends and the lobbies overflow with pot and passion, everyone seems embarrassed at how truly non-exclusive the raga has become. Even a year ago, you could lose yourself among all that curried suave at one of these affairs. But Ravi Shankar has absorbed a vast audience of love-beaded, soft-voiced kids who have all Ravi's records and can play his greatest hits on the electric sitar and wish they were old enough to attend the class he gives at City College.

Hip has become a masscult, and Ravi Shankar finds himself not the prophet of an elite but a universal guru. His followers want something so new and miraculous even Marshall McLuhan can't understand it. They don't want a mere Eastern exposure. They want Buddhahood on a long-play record, Tao on tap, a bath in the Ganges without getting wet. And they want Ravi Shankar (who studied 14 hours a day for seven years to learn the basics of raga) to sock it to them.

But he is no saran-wrap swami. He declares: "I have nothing to do with raga-rock." But he does not reject the form. "I do not think this music is ruining the sitar. It is like the guitar which is

used by classical musicians and also for folk and now popular music."

On the tenuous connection between acid-rock and raga, he says: "I have met a number of people who have been studying or indulging in that field. They are absolutely sure I am high whenever I play. I have never had any drug experience. I can only say, through use of discipline and yoga, drugs are not needed."

Ravi Shankar's pivotal place in the teenie underground became assured when George Harrison named him personal mentor. The master was not so sure at first that he wanted the honor. He met George at a dinner party last June. Though he had heard for some time that the Beatles were among his most ardent English admirers, he refused to consider their patronage anything more than a "gimmick." But he found Harrison "humble and sincere; he said he wanted to learn properly and I told him he must give up everything and start again from basics." George surprised everyone by following through on the suggestion, and he arrived in India complete with a bushy moustache. But the disguise proved inadequate. Every day, his bemused teacher regarded 2000 to 5000 teenagers screaming for their idol outside the hotel. Enraged, Harrison held a press conference to berate Indian youth for turning their backs on native music. Delighted elders had the text reprinted in all the papers, and suddenly the Beatles became traditionalists.

Harrison's conversion has given Ravi Shankar access to the elite in American pop music. He seems delighted at the reception but unwilling to reciprocate. Western musicians have not taught him anything, he insists. "The worlds of jazz, folk, and electronic music have all been influenced by our music because they found something they didn't already have. But Western music hasn't influenced me at all. We are so very much richer."

Ravi Shankar greets the great glance Eastward by glancing back. He is willing to play for deaf audiences who cry "bravo" when he tunes up. He is willing to sip coffee with tweedy creatures from the press. He is willing to teach a class on the rudiments of raga. And he is wiling to confront this latest frenzy, which calls itself a teenager, with the ease of somebody who has been where everything is going all along.

The teenie satori makes him smile. Five years ago a lot of people

thought his music sounded like a sick cat; now he packs 'em in in London and New York. Five years ago, they wondered why he didn't wear a turban; now they ask for his autograph. Five years ago, they called it an "ethnic" sound; now they write term papers about him and talk in hushed whispers about his vital infusion of rock 'n' roll.

Ravi Shanker sighs, smiles from the corners of his mouth, and tells those reporters gathered to hear his pronouncements about their youth: "Touch wood, we haven't had to borrow from other cultures. Our music grows within itself."

—THE VILLAGE VOICE, 1967

# THE HEAD FREAK AWAITS A NEW SON

The three-year-old kid answered the door, took a cool look at the policeman standing there, raised his full blue eyes and declared: "Fuck off, cop."

"Where's your folks, son?"

The kid brushed his white-cotton hair out of his eyes. It fell in swirling puffs down his shoulders. "Fuck off," he repeated, without blinking.

So, naturally, the policeman left.

The legend is one of many traveling the Los Angeles underground and concerning a sapling who struck like a wet branch and went by the name of Godo.

His father, one Vitautus Alphonsus Paulekas, is the chief of a vague tribe known as the Freaks. In the legend, Vito is part teacher, part artist, part dancer. His hands and feet are instruments of magic; his eyes are sorcerer's eyes.

Vito is not the most articulate of wizards, but he comes on booming like thunder. His theories make meager sense, but they are expounded with a galactic joy. His eyes jolt from briar patches of wrinkles, and there is a phosphorous giggle in every statement to let you know that behind the dogma is the laughing gas of experience.

His apartment, crammed below a gymnasium, has the look of a shrine. The living room is slung with webs of beads and drapery.

The bedroom is small and dark like the passage of a good-sized sewer; its only window is shrouded in leaded glass. The whole place resounds with canned patter from a radio turned up Up UP to compete with the bouncing medicine balls and bar-bells.

All over the house, on every wall, hang pictures of Godo immaculate. In the basement, where Vito teaches sculpture, work by father and son stands in a row along walls caked with clay. Godo's water colors run to bold resolute patterns. No merging shapes or colors—just simple, certain form. Vito's busts are leering, lipless people with gaping teeth and breasts. They are super-detailed, bug-eyed monsters crying out in Los Angelic terror.

The art of L.A., inherent in every brazen boulevard, celebrates the grotesque. These sun-baked Pacific people will have none of that Brancusi perfection in their sculpture, no breeze-like Calder mystery, no Giacometti bone-marrow angst.

Vito's scene could double as a set for one of those 1950 Hollywood exposes that took you behind the scenes into a "real" beatnik pad, where chicks danced bra-less to bongos while some collegiate-looking cat read poetry and smoked a jade pipe. He comes on like a living cliche, everybody's favorite beatnik. This adherence to form explains the attention Vito gets from filmmakers, TV producers, and editors of girlie magazines. He looks too much the rebel to be one. His familiar blend of Love-Work-Marxism actually renders him benign, and that is what we expect from artists. Vito is cast as a nut, and therefore tolerated. He has made frequent appearances on the Joe Pyne Show ("to establish communication with the people of Los Angeles") where he makes an ideal sparring partner. The rumored friendship between "Iconoclast Vito" and "Joe-the-Brute" is no coincidence; both are roles which seem too simple to be real.

So it comes as no surprise to learn of Vito's forays into exploitation. A skin magazine features a photo-spread about "a name that represents nonconformity, artistic freedom, originality . . . one of the most diversified sculptors the world has ever known." Vito is featured in films like *Girl On F Street* or *Mondo Bizarro*, neither of which will make them drool at the editorial office of *Cahiers Du Cinema*.

"Any publicity is good publicity," he reflects. "You go through

this routine with naked girls, and they pan over and show your sculpture. I believe in the object itself; once they show that, they can say anything."

If there were no Vito, the L.A.P.D. would have to invent him. His peculiar fraud is what the scene had made of him. He takes his wife Sue and his people (a group of 35 energized kids) and hops from club to club grooving with the city's best rock bands. To watch the tribe dance is a revelation. There are leaps and bounds, swaying strands of hair and bouncing, stomping feet. Sue moves like Fay Wray caught in some frenzied Kong-embrace; neck taut, shoulders erect, hair streaming free. In the center, Vito flays the smoky air and roars. It is pure, awkward energy because when Vito dances he lets his eyes take over his body, and all that glittering blue shows.

To the cops, Vito's people are the most brazen exponents of a lifestyle that is somewhere between reprehensible and forbidden. Teen culture demands of its heroes that they be a menace to adults and by simply being themselves the Freaks haunt straight Los Angeles. They have no penchant for destruction, but whenever the Freaks appear they cause such loathing terror in the general populace that they might as well be shouting "burn, baby, burn!"

Vito claims he is "the most checked-out man in this city," elaborating: "There are plainclothesmen in all my classes, and whenever we dance somewhere the management is threatened with all kinds of injunctions." His distaste for cops goes back a long way. At 18, he spent a year and a half in a reformatory and after that, he admits, he was busted a few more times. Vito's childhood is a hazy fairytale. He is the son of a Lithuanian sausage-maker who settled in Massachusetts. He recalls: "My father's fingers became shaped for stringing frankfurters. He used to walk home with sausages wrapped around his legs."

Vito's formal education encompassed four blurred years of his life. All he chooses to remember is an early love of sculpture. "I used to fool around with clay. While the other kids were busy learning to be useful citizens, I was building naked women."

His art succeeds whether or not it is valid because it is uniquely his. His dance technique needs no esthetic; it was perfected during Vito's career as a marathon dancer. "The marathon taught me

something important," he claims. "I had to place myself entirely in the possession of my partner for three hours. I carried her through the milkman's matinee and then she carried me. After six months of that kind of trust, I learned to let go completely."

Dancer, sculptor, dancer, scofflaw. He will never come of age, says the legend. His eyes will never wrinkle. It is beautiful to watch Sue and Vito play.

His son Godo was a child's child. *Life* magazine described him as "the most beautiful child in creation, with pure blond hair to his shoulders . . . pudgy little cheeks and blue eyes that are steady and make you want to weep."

In the midst of Vito's ugliest statuary stands an angelic bust of his son. It is a stylistic reversal: no torment, no suspicion, none of the envy-condemnation Vito feels and shows for the straight world. Just a father looking at his son.

"Every place he went, Godo had an intensity with every human being," says Vito. "He sized up people long before I did, and he would tell me about them. He made love to everybody."

Godo is central to the Freak mythology. He is Apollo-Jesus, golden boy, the realization, an expert drummer at two and a half.

But Godo is dead. It happened last December, on Vito's roof. Godo encountered a rusted trap door and started to play with it. It opened and he fell in. At the hospital, the doctors called it nothing serious and let Vito see his son. Godo lay strapped and spreadeagled on a metal table. A sterile towel covered the hole in his head. His fists were pale and clenched.

Vito opened his blue eyes wider than ever as his son cried over and over, "Help me."

An hour later, Godo had hemorrhaged and died. No earthquake, no fire-and-brimstone accompaniment, no final revelation. Just a real baby dying. Absurdity kills myths.

Recalling that day, Vito hardens, straightens, narrows. His wrinkled lids blink shut. "The D.A.'s office is trying to get something on me for this," he explains in spurts. "I heard from people in their office that they tried to find evidence of drugs on Godo's body. It wasn't a rotten trap door they were after; that's legal. But drugs . . ."

No one has to accuse Vito; the subject of responsibility comes

up by itself. Why wasn't a tracheotomy performed at the hospital? Why did they tie Godo down to a table? Why was the door left to rot?

"An old friend of mine came to see us afterward," Vito recalls. "She said: 'Vito, your baby is dead. God punished you for doing the things you did with him.'" Vito's laugh becomes a nervous giggle. "My son was killed by a bum trap door, not by any God," he demands. No one says anything. No one accuses. But Vito feels weight on his shoulders anyway. The head Freak of Los Angeles, the ultimate iconoclast, has his own superstition: God is punishing him for immeasurable evil. Godo is dead and God, in the form of a cop, isn't through with Vito yet.

But myths never die; they only transmigrate. Godo was necessary solder. He held the legend together. He was living proof: the second Freaky generation. So the underground awaits his resurrection and the occasion may not be far away. Sue is six months pregnant, and sewing clothes. A box of lacy nightshirts waits in anticipation.

"My baby is dancing already in Sue's belly," Vito exalts. "Sue was dancing right in this kitchen while she was in labor. When Godo was born he came out with his mouth already open, making noise."

The living legend has a new inspiration. A child messiah will be born among the Freaks. Lightning will strike Beverly Hills. Thunderbolts will shatter over Sacramento. Sunset Strip will hiss, crack, and split. Chief Vito's sorcerer's eyes will twinkle as—amid the stucco ruins—Godo is risen.

—NEW YORK MAGAZINE, 1967

# THE SHAMAN AS SUPERSTAR

"The shaman . . . he was a man who would intoxicate himself. See, he was probably already an . . . uh . . . unusual individual. And, he would put himself into a trance by dancing, whirling around, drinking, taking drugs—however. Then, he would go on a mental travel and . . . uh . . . describe his journey to the rest of the tribe."

JIM MORRISON

He comes to meet you in superstar fatigues: a slept-in pullover and the inevitable leather pants. A lumpy hat covers most of his mane. You mutter "groovy" at each other in greeting, and split for the beach. His most recent song comes on the radio. You both laugh as he turns up the volume, and fiddles with the bass controls. It's a perfect afternoon, so he picks up his girl. She says, "Your hat makes you look like a Rembrandt, Jim," and he whispers, "Oh, wow," riding the image as though it were a breaking wave.

Between freeways, you talk about his bust in New Haven (the charge: indecent and immoral exhibition), the war, psychoanalysis, and his new album. He wants to call it "The Celebration of the Lizard" after a 24-minute "drama" which he has just composed. He is very much into reptiles. He wants the album's jacket printed in pseudo-snakeskin, with its title embossed in gold.

The official interview takes place in a sequestered inlet at the Garden of Self-Realization, an ashram Hollywood style. You sit

not far from an urn certified to contain Mahatma Gandhi's ashes. Music is piped in from speakers at the top of a stucco arch with cupolas sprayed gold. The ground on which you are assembling your tape recorder is filled with worms. They seem to be surfacing around his hands, and he examines one as you set the mike in place. A willing suppliant, it lies prone upon his palm. Does it know him as a serpent-king?

Amid a burst of strings from the hidden speakers, you ask the trial question. Jim answers in a slithering baritone. "I dunno . . . I haven't thought about it." The garden supplies Muzak hosannas.

"When you started, did you anticipate your image?"

"Nahhh. It just sort of happened . . . unconsciously."

"How did you prepare yourself for stardom?"

"Uh . . . about the only thing I did was . . . I stopped getting haircuts."

"How has your behavior onstage changed?"

"See, it used to be . . . I'd just stand still and sing. Now, I . . . uh . . . exaggerate a little bit."

His voice drops an octave at the sight of a tape recorder, and the surrogate audience it represents. He gives a cautious mischievous interview, contemplating each question as though it were a hangnail, and answering with just a trace of smile in the corners of his quotation marks. But he gets his scene across.

"I'm beginning to think it's easier to scare people than to make them laugh."

"I wonder why people like to believe I'm high all the time. I guess . . . maybe they think someone else can take their trip for them."

"A game is a closed field . . . a ring of death with . . . uh . . . sex at the center. Performing is the only game I've got, so . . . I guess it's my life."

His statements, like his songs, are unpunctuated puzzles. You connect the dots between images, and become involved. "I'm a word man," he exults. In discussing his craft, he sputters with esthetic energy. "See, there's this theory about the nature of tragedy, that Aristotle didn't mean catharsis for the audience, but a purgation of emotions for the actors themselves. The audience is just a witness to the event taking place onstage."

He suggests you read Nietzsche on the nature of tragedy to understand where he is really at. His eyes glow as he launches into a discussion of the Apollonian-Dionysian struggle for control of the life force. No need to guess which side he's on.

"See, singing has all the things I like," he explains. "It's involved with writing and with music. There's a lot of acting. And it has this one other thing . . . a physical element . . . a sense of the immediate. When I sing, I create characters."

"What kinds of characters?"

"Oh . . . hundreds. Hundreds of 'em."

*"I like to think he just arrived—*
*you know, came out of nowhere"*
A FAN

He was born James Douglas Morrison, under the sign of Sagittarius the hunter, in Melbourne, Florida, 24 years ago. He once told a reporter, "You could say I was ideally suited for the work I'm doing. It's the feeling of a bow string being pulled back for 22 years and suddenly let go."

But he won't discuss those years on the taut end of existence. He would like you to accept his appearance as a case of spontaneous generation—America's love-lion spurting full grown from the neon lions of the '60s. "They claim everyone was born, but I don't remember it," he insists. "Maybe I was having one of my blackouts."

To accept the thumbnail sketch he offers, there is little in Jim's past to account for his presence. His father is an admiral, but he doesn't think that explains his fascination with authority or his devotion to its overthrow. His family moved so often that his most immediate childhood memories are of landscapes. But that suggests nothing to him about his current shiftlessness. (He lives in motels, or with friends.)

Jim parries questions about his personal experience with acrobatic agility. You find yourself wondering whether he can manipulate his soul with the same consummate ease. Does he choose to show an amiable crescent of himself for this interview? Does his dark side appear at random, or can he summon the lunatic within the way most of us put on a telephone voice? You keep trying to catch him in a moment of prefabricated magic (he wouldn't be

the first shaman to take refuge in ritual). But any attempt to grasp the corporeal essence of Jim Morrison is repelled by that fortress of ego, which is yet another of his persona. Behind the walls, however, you sense a soft, slippery kid, who was probably lonely and certainly bored.

"I was a good student. Read a lot. But I was always . . . uh . . . talking when I wasn't supposed to. They made me sit at a special table . . . nothing bad enough to get kicked out, of course. I got through school . . . Went to Florida State University . . . mainly because . . . I couldn't think of anything else to do."

He came west after college to attend the U.C.L.A. film school. He lived alone in Venice, among the muddy canals and peeling colonnades. The roof of a deserted warehouse was his office. He spent most of his free time there, writing and planning a career in the literary underground. He was brooding (now they say "intense") and shy (in the fan magazines, "sensitive"). A classmate recalls: "He was a lot like he is now, but nobody paid much attention then."

At U.C.L.A., Morrison met Ray Manzarek, a young filmmaker and a jazz pianist on the side. For a while they shared a tiny flat, and Jim began to share his poems as well. It was Manzarek who thought of setting them to music. And though he had never sung before, Jim spent the next few months exploring his voice, and transmitting his vision to drummer John Densmore and guitarist Robbie Krieger. They added sturdy hinges to the sound of the Doors. With Manzarek skimming the keyboard of an electric organ like a flat pebble on water, the new group was tight and sinewy from the start. They did bread-gigs at small clubs along the Sunset Strip, reworking rock-blues standards and staking out a milieu for themselves. But they spent most of their dormant period implementing the controlled insanity that Jim Morrison was soon to loose on modern rock. Long before the three musical Doors ever saw the inside of a recording studio, they had distilled the essence of Jim's screaming "recitatif" into vibrant rhythms and riffs.

"We all play a lead and subjugation things with each other," explains Ray. "When Jim gets into something, I'm able to give of that area within myself. We may look cool, but we are really evil, insidious cats behind Jim. We instigate the violence in him. A lot

of times he doesn't feel particularly angry but the music just drives him to it."

This total immersion of sentiment in sound amplifies Morrison's lyrics, transforming them into something more like pageant than poetry. Jim himself is ennobled by the sound. Onstage, his voice becomes a fierce rattle, and all his games are magic spells. In a tiny sweat-cellar like Ondine, where they first played in New York: magic. In the Singer Bowl in Flushing, where they play on August 2. On the radio. In stereophonic sound: magic. They put a spell on you.

*"Think of us as erotic politicians."*

JIM MORRISON to *Newsweek*

Elvis Presley was the Rasputin of Rock. He ground country funk into the nation's consciousness by playing music as though it were motion. Even with his famous hips obscured on television, there was magic in every quiver of his voice.

Presley's hillbilly grace is now a patriarchal paunch. But none of the rock titans who followed him has inherited his crown. Even the Beatles built their empire on clean energy ("Yeah, yeah, yeah") and later refined that base through the safe profundity of artsong. The Rolling Stones came close. Their message was the ecstasy of straight potent sex, and their medium was honest ugliness. But the Stones were after mere rape, not soul plunder.

The Doors, however, are an inner theatre of cruelty. Their musical dramas have made fear and trembling part of the rock lexicon. These days every band worth its psychedelic salt has a local lunatic singing lead. But the Doors have already transcended their own image. Now, they are in search of total sensual contact with an audience. They may yet appear at a future concert in masks. As Ray Manzarek explains: "We want our music to shortcircuit the conscious mind and allow the subconscious to flow free."

That goal is a realization of all that was implicit in Elvis Presley's sacred wiggle. But if Elvis was an unquestioning participant in his own hysteria, the Doors celebrate their myth as a creative accomplishment. Playing sorcerer is Jim's thing—not a job, or a hobby, or even one of those terribly necessary rituals we sanctify with the name Role. Jim calls it "play":

"Play is not the same thing as a game," he explains. "A game involves rules. But play is an open event. It's free. Like, you know how people walk to where they're going—very orderly, right? But little kids . . . they're like dogs. They run around, touch things, sing a song. Well, actors play like that. Also, musicians. And you dig watching somebody play, because that's the way human beings are supposed to be . . . free. Like animals."

Words are Jim's playpen. He jots stanzas, images, and allusions into a leather bound notebook, as they occur to him. These are shaped and sifted into the thought-collages which are the Doors' finished lyrics.

> . . . Awkward instant
> And the first animal is jettisoned,
> Legs furiously pumping
> Their stiff green gallop,
> And heads bob up
> Poise
> Delicate
> Pause
> Consent
> In mute nostril agony. . . .*

"See, this song is called 'Horse Latitudes' because it's about the Doldrums, where sailing ships from Spain would get stuck. In order to lighten the vessel, they had to throw things overboard. Their major cargo was working horses for the New World. And this song is about that moment when the horse is in air. I imagine it must have been hard to get them over the side. When they got to the edge, they probably started chucking and kicking. And it must have been hell for the men to watch, too. Because horses can swim for a while, but then they lose their strength and just go down . . . slowly sink away."

Even when Jim writes about impersonal situations they become charged with the tension of imminent explosion. Violence is his major motif. It permeates to the core of his work. His central symbol, the Great Snake, appears throughout the repertory of the Doors. Sometimes it is a phallic liberator, extolling an act of

creative desecration. Sometimes it is a handy fetish to wave in the breeze, instead of the real thing. But most often, it is the agent of self-knowledge, residing in our imaginations, and slinking toward consciousness to be born. Most Doors songs plead with us to reject all repressive authority and embrace the Great Snake, with its slippery equation of freedom and violence. It is an equation we are eager to make, rendering holy what is simply unrestrained.

*"Robbie and I were sittin' on a plane an' like it's first class, so you get a couple o' drinks, an' I said to Robbie, 'Y'know, there are these Apollonian people . . . like, very formal, rational dreamers. An' then there's the Dionysian thing . . . the insanity trip . . . way inside.' An' I said, 'You're an Apollonian . . . up there with your guitar . . . all neat an' thought out . . . y'know . . . an' you should get into the Dionysian thing.'*

*"An' he looks up at me an' says, 'Oh, yeah, right Jim.' "*

The Lizard King slithers down Sunset Strip in a genuine snake-skin jacket and leather tights. Bands of teenyboppers flutter about like neon butterflies, but he is oblivious to their scene. He moves past ticky-tacoramas and used-head shops into the open arms of recording studio B, where his true subjects wait.

He greets us with a grin out of "Thus Spake Zarathustra," and we realize instantly that Jim is loaded. Juiced. Stoned—the old way. Booze. No one is surprised; Jim is black Irish to the breath. He deposits a half-empty quart bottle of wine on top of the control panel and downs the remnants of somebody's beer.

"Hafta' break it in," he mutters, caressing the sleeves of his jacket. It sits green and scaly on his shoulders, and crinkles like tinfoil whenever he moves.

"It's—very Tennessee Williams, Jim."

Grunt. He turns to producer Paul Rothchild with a spacious grin that says, "I'm here, so you can start." But Rothchild makes little clicking noises with his tongue. He is absorbed in a musical problem, and he offers only a perfunctory nod to the tipsy titan at his side.

Behind a glass partition three musical Doors hunch over their instruments, intent on a rhythm line that refuses to render itself

whole. The gap between Morrison and the other Doors is vast in the studio, where the enforced cohesion of live performance is missing. On their own, they are methodic musicians. Densmore drums in sharp, precise strokes. Krieger's guitar undulates like a belly dancer—sinuous but sober. And at the organ, Manzarek is cultivated and crisp. With his shaggy head atop a pair of plywood shoulders, he looks like a hip undertaker.

Jim walks into the studio and accosts a vacant mike. He writhes in languid agony, jubilant at the excuse to move in his new jacket. But Rothchild keeps the vocal mike dead, to assure maximum concentration on the problem at hand. From behind the glass partition, Jim looks like a silent movie of himself, speeded up for laughs. The musicians barely bother to notice. When he is drinking, they work around him. Only Ray is solicitous enough to smile. The others tolerate him, as a pungent but necessary prop.

"I'm the square of the Western hemisphere," he says, returning to his wine. "Man . . . whenever somebody'd say something groovy . . . it'd blow my mind. Now, I'm learnin'. . . . You like people? I hate 'em . . . screw 'em . . . I don't need 'em . . . Oh, I need 'em . . . to grow potatoes."

He teeters about the tiny room, digging his boots into the carpeting. Between belches, he gazes at each of us, smirking as though he has found something vaguely amusing behind our eyes. But the seance is interrupted when Rothchild summons him. While Jim squats behind the control panel, a roughly recorded dub of his "Celebration of the Lizard" comes over the loudspeakers.

Gently, almost apologetically, Ray tells him the thing doesn't work. Too diffuse, too mangy. Jim's face sinks beneath his scaly collar. Right then, you can sense that "The Celebration of the Lizard" will never appear on record—certainly not on the new Doors album. There will be eleven driving songs, and snatches of poetry, read aloud the way they do it at the 92nd St. Y. But no Lizard-King. No Monarch crowned with love beads and holding the phallic scepter in his hand.

"Hey, bring your notebook to my house tomorrow morning, okay?" Rothchild offers.

"Yeah." Jim answers with the look of a dog who's just been told he's missed his walk. "Sure."

Defeated, the Lizard King seeks refuge within his scales. He disappears for ten minutes and returns with a bottle of brandy. Thus fortified, he closets himself inside an anteroom used to record isolated vocals. He turns the lights out, fits himself with earphones, and begins his game.

Crescendos of breath between the syllables. His song is half threat, and half plea:

> Five to one baby
> One in five
> Nobody here
> Gets out alive . . .*

Everyone in the room tries to bury Jim's presence in conversation. But his voice intrudes, bigger and blacker than life, over the loudspeakers. Each trace of sound is magnified, so we can hear him guzzling and belching away. Suddenly, he emerges from his formica cell, inflicting his back upon a wall, as though he were being impaled. He is sweat-drunk, but still coherent, and he mutters so everyone can hear: "If I had an axe . . . man, I'd kill everybody . . .'xept . . . uh . . . my friends."

Sagittarius the hunter stalks us with his glance. We sit frozen, waiting for him to spring.

"Ah—I hafta get one o' them Mexican wedding shirts," he sighs.

Robbie's girl, Donna, takes him on: "I don't know if they come in your size."

"I'm a medium . . . with a large neck."

"We'll have to get you measured, then."

"Uh-uh . . . I don't like to be measured." His eyes glow with sleep and swagger.

"Oh Jim, we're not gonna measure all of you. Just your shoulders."

—NEW YORK MAGAZINE, 1968

# III
# SEENS

# ● THE PSYCHEDELIC PSELL

Okay.

You've swallowed the magic cube, downed a cup of "organic" tea with filigree leaves, and placed the diamond needle on the appropriate sounds.

Now sit back and wait 20 minutes, until twinges of nausea herald the coming of the hereafter.

Meanwhile, ponder this:

A discotheque called The World advertises "psychedelic beauty contests." Admen chortle: "Don't blow your cool—blow your mind." Bosley Crowther calls *The Fantastic Voyage* "quite a trip." Albert Zugsmith's successor to *Fanny Hill* is a movie called *LSD—I Hate You*. They photographed *Kaleidoscope* in "Psychedelic color." *The Cabinet of Dr. Caligari* has been advertised as: "The original psychedelic filmic trip."

Psychedelic shoes. Acid TV commercials. LSD greeting cards. Marijuana brownies. Mandala shopping bags. Tibetan cocktails on the rocks. "Psychedelicize suburbia." Mind-expanding peacock feathers. Buddha himself, gold and grinning, comes embossed on a 100 percent washable cotton sweatshirt in assorted sizes, colors, and cools.

As the music sharpens into neon-ness, as the room thickens like tapioca, ask yourself this: What about the prophet's profits?

Timothy Leary's name appears in a mass circulation magazine

103

or two every week. His records are being rushed to outlets all over the country. He turns out introductions to other people's books the way Japanese craftsmen produce tin Statues of Liberty. Currently, he's writing his memoirs. He brings his caftan and his charisma to the Merv Griffin show. He locks in fierce debate with Alan Burke, and wins on the strength of his forgiving cool. He holds press conferences at the Advertising Club on Park Avenue. And, if half the rumors are true, he turns on: doctors, lawyers, publishers, artists, policemen, senators, and—by his own implication—Presidents-to-be.

In New York's second largest theatre, he also runs a religion. When the Federal Government chose to arrest Timothy Leary for leaving the country while a "narcotics offender," they merely convinced an additional few hundred people that the Village Theatre was *the* place to be on Tuesday nights. The government is Leary's most generous patron; they shower him with the raw material for martyrdom. He already turns on the beautiful people, but the Narcs are helping Leary reach the guys who guzzle beer.

Along Second Avenue Leary acknowledges the greetings of admirers like a Zen Rockefeller. He folds his hands together and bows his head in the direction of a compliment. His eyes close slightly, and his mouth spreads in a quiescent, comprehensive smile.

In the delicatessen on 7th Street, a middle-aged waitress recognizes the good Doctor and dries her hands on an apron to serve him. "Have I got a pastrami sandwich for you," she chortles. When it arrives, she thrusts it toward him with a flourish and, as Leary pours his beer, takes it back again. "Who gave you that corned beef?" she scowls. "Pastrami is juicier; you get pastrami."

Leary munches his sandwich and gets into his concept-thing.

"It's going to take at least one generation to come to terms with LSD."

The waitress beams.

"This is a transition generation. When you think of the history of new movements, no culture has been so tolerant of a force that's going to wipe it out as America. In any other time or place we'd be in danger of our lives."

The cook comes out of his kitchen for a peek.

"Imagine an LSD revolution in China."

Reaching Dr. Leary for an interview is no longer as easy as dialing 914 and the appropriate Millbrook digits. Ever since the League for Spiritual Discovery premiered its "psychedelic celebrations," you have to go through the box office, the booking agent, a public relations man, and a manager who tells you to "be sure and mention his assistants; they haven't been getting the publicity they should."

But it's still easy enough to pop into the theatre on Tuesday afternoon when the League holds dress rehearsals. Workmen sweep in the aisles, oblivious to the revolution. Stone cherubs and flourishes frame the kinetic fireworks on stage.

"The theatre has been taken over by careerist intellectuals," Leary says. "It has to be returned to its original motive. Plays by Tennessee Williams, for instance, are the memoirs of a neurotic, not art. Art must involve the senses. All original drama is psychedelic. The theatre, remember, was originally a religious experience. It all stems back to religious motives—someone with a vision turns other people on. That's why we're proud to be packing 'em in down here."

The show is damned good theatre. Above and beyond the ideology. Jackie Cassen and Rudi Stern prove themselves to be masters of the mixed-media form. Their re-enactment of the birth-life-death of Harry Haller is as sharp as cut glass in the mind. Colors and lines swirl through space and dimension. Shapes and sounds pulsate in a glowing whirlpool. Shadows of apish men copulate against a ragafied background.

With "The Death of the Mind," Leary's metaphysics of theatre become more than theory. Getting the point of the Cassen-Stern lightshow is a matter of instinct. Bring along a McLuhanistic frame of reference and you'll miss it. Leary is aware of media criticism, though he insists: "McLuhan knows about psychedelic art but he's all external; he hasn't seen the inside yet. It'll be fascinating to see what happens when he takes LSD."

Harry Haller's trip—from turn on, to sensory pleasure, to ego-games, to an archetypal vision—follows ALL the rules of acid-sensuality until he encounters the nub of his hostility: the wolf of the steppes.

The contemplation ends abruptly. Leary's show reaches a classic

denouement, when Haller strangles his soul-guru. Though the
Doctor assures us that Harry will work out his hostility through
purgative laughter, we are left suspended in Harry's trip. Like the
old Saturday serials, with Buck Rogers hanging over an interstellar
laser beam, we are told: Turn on, tune in, drop out, next week,
same time, same place.

Cassen and Stern took five months to create the visuals for "The
Death of the Mind." They worked with a miniature theatre at Millbrook, using 15 machines and a series of complexly painted slides
and mandalas. Rudi Stern says of his work in intermedia: "What
we're doing is a return to basic forms in theatre, to shadow play.
Artaud first envisioned a theatre taking the form of mythic structure—light, sound, and shadow replacing narrative, pantomime
replacing acting. It's all a very pure thing."

The psychedelic faith draws from an abundance of ideology
like this. But, beyond the core, Timothy Leary's big apple is rotting
away. As the lines grow outside the Village Theatre, as the testimonials multiply and the evidence mounts that Leary's cause, if
not his case, may actually hold together, acid culture is going the
way of all ideology which succeeds. The gurus have been too busy
chewing to notice that the beast they are devouring is gnawing away
in return. In subverting mass culture from the inside, they too have
become a collection of instant-antique Americana. As Madison
Avenue becomes hip and turned on to LSD, our commercials are
beginning to assimilate the accouterments of acid-faith. The glut
of psychedelightful and psychedelicious goodies on sale in the pages
of the underground press is one legacy of Timothy Leary's gospel.
If fact follows fashion, we should soon be witnessing the Mac-
Dougalization of acid art on the streets of San Francisco, the glens
of collegiate America, and finally, on the radios and televisions of
our collective imaginations. Pop culture emanates spokelike from
New York. Right now, acid art is where pop art was three years
ago—a penthouse passion. The banning of acid-rock on the radio
already seems futile next to its warm acceptance by the advertising
media. The psychedelic experience is being mass-propagated right
now—but without the commitment. It is probably no fault of the
gospel that its ultimate turn-on to America will come in the form
of colored patterns on boxes of breakfast food. But the blood and

body are being drained from Timothy Leary's eucharist and—in a mercantile transubstantiation—are being mass-produced as love beads. There is no Judas in Leary's garden of Gethsemane; treason is within the prophet himself.

Jackie Cassen protests: "We don't consider this commercialized. This has nothing to do with distribution. We're involved in a religious celebration here." But Cassen and Stern reproduce the psychedelic experience in the very-secularized church at Cheetah. They did the lighting for the Byrds' recent gig at the Village Gate. *Time* magazine says of their work: "boffo." And a large ad in *Variety* boasts: "They can convert any room into a kaleidoscopic world of movement, light, and color (and they'll do it so you've got enough left over in your budget for a new set of china). They can turn a sagging club into the hottest spot in town . . . Jackie Cassen and Rudi Stern (available) for discotheque, fashion shows, ballet, industrial shows, commercials, bar mitzvahs."

Kinetic kreplach? Mind-manifesting matzah?

The one thing the psychedelic religion has neglected to do is to publicly chase the money changers from its temple. It shows. It obscures the art of Cassen and Stern. It makes the line outside the Village Theatre seem like a theatre party from Jackson Heights. It makes Timothy Leary a tax deduction.

Any journalist who listens to the quiet assurance of triumph ("The police state mentality always attempts to repress sensory experience; it never works"), the plans ("Our design is to educate as well as turn on . . . we open in California this January"), and the awareness ("Any form of energy can be misused by fools and villains. We're trying to teach people to take it seriously; the average man has got to come to his senses") faces a formidable problem. In a city of gilded hoaxes, the hair which falls graying over Timothy Leary's eyes, the round green marble eyes, the encrusted bird-dung on his sweater, are they all part of the same game?

That's why Timothy Leary needs a new kind of public relations. The time has come for the guru to draw a line between revelation and merchandising.

There are already signs of precocious in-fighting along the psychedelic front. One of Leary's close associates calls the Warhol-Velvet Underground format: "just an amphetamine scene." And

the answer from the Factory goes like this: "Timothy Leary couldn't be serious; he's Irish." The Off Off-Broadway circuit is slicing up the acid-pie in a brilliant little parody called "Psychedelic Follies." There are bitter references to "the Reverend Timothy Leary." The good Doctor may find himself a Catholic for the second time, as one apostle or another plasters a manifesto over the marquee of the Village Theatre and ushers in the reformation.

Timothy Leary has until the first psychedelic Ban Roll-On commercial to do something about all this.

—THE VILLAGE VOICE, 1967

# THE POLITICS OF
# SALVATION

The question of the hour is: can an honest man still be a fraud?

The Maharishi Mahesh Yogi arrived in New York fresh from triumphs in all the pop capitals of the West. The Beatles sent pink tulips and carnations to his suite at the Plaza. The Beach Boys— long fascinated by mystic meditation—accompanied him from Los Angeles. And the New York press establishment greeted him with equal measures of suspicion and relief. They were, after all, tired of the hippies.

On Friday morning, he received reporters in the Plaza's State Suite, a generous room decorated in Versailles Nouveau. Chic ladies and gentlemen from the fashion slicks scurried around television cables for a glimpse of the guru's smile. Hippies with credentials formed a beaded wedge along the gold draperies. The ballsier reporters squatted around a white satin couch on which the Maharishi was sitting. His reflection filled every piece of crystal in the chandelier.

The Maharishi is a practical man. That is the only defense he offers for his particular meditative technique. "Maybe, it works," he shrugs at the end of a lecture, leaving his audience to ponder their needs and alternatives. And in organizing his Spiritual Regeneration Movement, he has shown the same sense of transcendent pragmatism. While his eventual plans call for universal participation, he extends an immediate invitation to the "fortunate possessors

of resources." He wants to train one teacher for every population of 100,000. This network of sub-gurus would be composed almost entirely of people who are powerful, important, or rich.

The Maharishi makes no attempt to disguise his elitism. He considers wealth and achievement important signs of spiritual advancement. Success, he reasons, is the logical result of inner peace, and failure cannot occur except through inner strife. Thus, he who is wealthy is usually healthy and potentially wise.

Wherever he has gone, the Maharishi has taken his movement to the taste-makers. In London, he found the Beatles; in San Francisco, the Grateful Dead; in Hollywood, a bevy of searching starlets. When he brought his technique to Germany, der guru approached factory bosses; after they discovered that transcendental meditation could increase production, they embraced the movement as a national asset.

In New York, the Maharishi wanted to meet the media. A theatrical agency, which also handles public relations for the Ringling Brothers, Barnum and Bailey Circus, arranged his press conference. They circulated in the audience with flowers in their stiff lapels, and surrounded their client like steel-gray columns.

"Jesus didn't have any public relations men around him," noted one reporter. "That is why he took so many hundreds of years to be known," the Maharishi replied in a small, tinkling voice. He cradled a hyacinth bud in one hand and gestured with the other. His eyes shone under the klieg lights like sunny water.

"Your Holiness, do you ever suffer?"

"I don't remember the last time I was depressed."

"Your Holiness, nine years ago you left your hermit's cave in the Himalayas. Why did you leave?"

"To come out."

"Your Majesty, how old are you?"

"As you look at me."

"What do your beads symbolize . . . what did you do for the Beatles . . . was your father a wise man?"

"He must have been."

"What did he do?"

"Work . . . as all men."

"Ahh, he's not gonna tell you."

The Maharishi does not enjoy talking about himself. When a personal question arises, his smile dims to a perplexed frown. He usually circumvents his own history, but he is reported to be about 56 years old, the son of a government revenue collector named Mahesh (Maharishi means great sage, and a yogi is a teacher). He is a university graduate who worked in a factory before he became a holy man. In recent days, his cave has been replaced by a palatial ashram with soundproof walls and indirect lighting.

Such luxury has caused widespread resentment against the Maharishi among India's holy men. But his place under the pleasure dome is still uncertain. He does seem to approve of any action which brings fulfillment ("If we are given the ability to have desires," he says, "why should we not also have the right to realize them?"). He rebukes religious leaders for their attempts to control and dogmatize experience ("Control has been found damaging to life. It is opposed to evolution and change"). And a hefty chunk of his lecture is always devoted to reconciling spiritual with material gain ("How is it possible for a man not to be material; the whole body is material").

But this unstructured approach does not extend to the Maharishi's personal system of meditation, which is a ritualized, if abstract procedure. His most publicized accomplishment has been the conversion of acidheads (something neither Billy Graham nor J. Edgar Hoover could achieve). Although he has never suggested that drugs are evil—only unnecessary—his followers seem to relish the "evolutionary" aspect of turning straight. Audiences at his talks are urged not to smoke. If that does not sound like the bidding of an epicurean, neither does vegetarianism, and yet the Maharishi eats no meat.

Finally, though he ministers to the elect, he vehemently denies an interest in amassing personal wealth. Questions about money make him almost sad. After a few jibes from the press last Friday, he quipped: "I am a monk and a monk has no pockets."

But the reporters chose to dwell on mercenary matters, and their concern was not entirely unprovoked. With a chuckle in his voice, the Maharishi answered a random question about poverty in India by explaining that the poor were lazy. A soft gasp—something like the deflation of a helium balloon—followed when he

added: "The hungry of India, China, anywhere, are lazy because of their lack of self-knowledge. We will teach them to derive from within, and then they will find food."

In the back of the room, a reporter with a sleek razor cut and a yellow rose in his lapel pondered the dynamics of transcendental deprivation. "Do we have to ignore the poor to achieve inner peace?" he asked.

"Like a tree in the middle of a garden, should we be liberal and allow the water to flow to other trees, or should we drink ourselves and be green?"

"But isn't this selfish?"

"Be absolutely selfish. That is the only way to bring peace, to be selfish, and if one does not have peace, how is one to help others attain it?"

With a smile and a syllogism, he was kindling the logs on his own pyre. The New York press establishment—on the reportorial level anyway—is a liberal-leaning body with a strong social orientation. Suddenly, the guru's words sounded like too many editorials in the *Daily News*. The cynic's mask that reporters wear so well slipped easily over most of the faces in that room after the Maharishi revealed that he was "no more interested in Vietnam than anywhere else in the world." He called Lyndon Johnson a peacemaker, to the imperceptible slamming of inner doors. A public relations man hastily called an end to the questioning just as the Maharishi announced that the Beach Boys would accompany him on his next nationwide tour. Even Walter Winchell would have winced.

But the Maharishi's press reception says more about our own preconceptions of holy men from the East than it does about the value of transcendental meditation. Since when does a social progressive make a better guru? Do we have the right to demand that our messiahs be democrats as well? Are we so certain that Jesus was a socialist?

Ultimately, the worth of any movement must be measured in its disciples. What is disturbing is not the Maharishi's Dale Carnegie approach to the politics of salvation. A man who thinks he has found the truth seldom worries about the context in which it is pronounced. But his followers—the rock stars, the post-hippies, the

student radicals, and the underground—must take the blame for letting "truth" come before reality.

They must know that this country is facing its most impolite summer in more than 100 years. Are we to teach the National Guard bliss consciousness so they can perform their duties with inner peace? Are we to meditate between strafings? Can we ever transcend America?

That is the solution this year's guru offers. He belongs on the cover of *Life-Look*. His message is one we are desperate to believe: that guilt is a futile emotion. "My heart is bouncing with bliss," he said to a capacity crowd at the Felt Forum of the New Madison Square Garden. "It is this afternoon that I am to announce without a doubt that transcendental meditation, if carried throughout the world, will create peace for generations to come."

In the audience, teenyboppers who had heard him on the radio and matrons who had seen him with Johnny Carson sighed and smiled at the small man amid the chrysanthemums. A middle-aged lady in a see-through dress and white go-go boots folded her hands in gratitude.

Can an honest man still be a fraud? If he allows himself to fill a fraudulent role—yes.

—THE VILLAGE VOICE, 1968

# ● SAN FRANCISCO BRAY

The most fragile thing to maintain in our culture is an underground. No sooner does a new tribe of rebels skip out, flip out, trip out, and take its stand, than photographers from *Life-Look* are on the scene doing cover layout. No sooner is a low-rent, low harassment quarter discovered than it appears in eight-color spreads on America's breakfast table. The need for the farther-out permeates our artistic involvement. American culture is a store window which must be periodically spruced and re-dressed. The new bohemians needn't worry about opposition these days; just exploitation. The handwriting on the wall says: preserve your thing.

The new music from San Francisco, most of it unrecorded at this writing, is the most potentially vital in the pop world. It shoots a cleansing wave over the rigid studiousness of rock. It brings driving spontaneity to a music that is becoming increasingly conscious of form and influence rather than effect. It is a resurgence which could drown the castrati who make easy listening and devour all those one-shot wonders floating above stagnant water.

Talent scouts from a dozen major record companies are now grooving with the tribes at the Fillmore and the Avalon. Hip San Francisco is being carved into bits of business turf. The Jefferson Airplane belong to RCA. The Grateful Dead has signed with Warner Brothers in an extraordinary deal which gives them complete control over material and production. Moby Grape is tinker-

ing with Columbia. And a bulge fistful of local talent is being wined and dined like the last available *shikse* in the promised land.

All because San Francisco is the Liverpool of the West. Not many bread-men understand the electronic rumblings from beneath the Golden Gate. But youth power still makes the pop industry move, and record executives know a fad sometimes needs no justification for success except its presence in a void. There is the feeling now, as pop shepherds watch the stars over their grazing flock, that if the San Francisco sound isn't the next Messiah, it will at least give the profits a run for their money.

"The important thing about San Francisco rock 'n' roll," says Ralph Gleason, "is that the bands here all sing and play live, and not for recordings. You get a different sound at a dance, it's harder and more direct."

Gleason, jazz and pop-music critic for *The San Francisco Chronicle,* writes with all the excitement of a participant. But he maintains the detachment of 20 years' experience. It is as though Bosley Crowther had set up headquarters at Warhol's Factory. Gleason's comprehension of the new sound is no small factor in its growth and acceptance by the hip establishment.

That Ralph Gleason writes from San Francisco is no coincidence. This city's rapport with the source of its ferment is unique. Traveling up the coast from the ruins of the Sunset Strip to the Haight is a Dantesque ascent. Those 400 miles mark the difference between a neon wasteland and the most important underground in the nation. San Francisco has the vanguard because it works hard to keep it. Native culture is cherished as though the city's consuming passion were to produce a statement that could not possibly be duplicated in New York. Chauvinism in Southern California runs to rhetoric about pulse and plastic, but up north it is have-you-seen-the-Mime-Troupe? and Haight-Street-makes-Greenwich-Village-look-like-a-city-dump.

Ten years ago, San Franciscans frowned on North Beach, but let it happen. Now, the city is prepared to support the rock underground by ignoring it. The theory of tacit neglect means a de facto tolerance of psychedelic drugs. San Francisco is far and away the most turned-on city in the Western world. "The cops are aware of

the number of heads here," says Bill Graham who owns the Fillmore and manages the Jefferson Airplane. "The law thinks it will fade out, like North Beach: What can they do? To see a cop in the Haight . . . it's like the English invading China. Once they own it, how are they going to police it?"

With safety in numbers, the drug and rock undergrounds swim up the same stream. The psychedelic ethic—still germinating and still unspoken—runs through the musical mainstream in a stiff current. When Bob Wier, rhythm guitarist of the Grateful Dead, says "the whole scene is like a contact high," he is not talking metaphor. Musical ideas are passed from group to group like a joint. There is an almost visible cohesion about San Francisco rock. With a scene that is small enough to navigate and big enough to make waves, with an establishment that all but provides the electric current, no wonder San Francisco is Athens. This acropolis has been carefully, sturdily built, and it is not going to crumble because nobody wants to see ruins messing up the skyline.

"I didn't have any musical revelation when I took acid. I'm a musician first. My drug experiences are separate. . . ." The speaker is a member of the Jefferson Airplane, the most established group in the Bay area.

Drugs are an open subject out here. When references appear in the music, they are direct and specific. But though concern with the dynamics of turning on is the most visible aspect of the scene here, it is by no means central to the music. While some groups seem impaled on a psychedelic spear ("How do we talk about drugs without getting banned from the radio?" is a key question of every Byrds album), San Francisco music says "pot" and goes on to other things. Bob Wier of the Grateful Dead insists: "We're not singing psychedelic drugs, we're singing music. We're musicians, not dope fiends."

He sits in the dining room of the three-story house he shares with the group, their women, and their community. The house is one of those masterpieces of creaking, curving spaciousness the Haight is filled with. Partially because of limited funds, but mostly because of the common consciousness which almost every group here adapts as its ethos, the Grateful Dead live and work together.

They are acknowledged as the best group in the Bay Area. Leader Jerry Garcia is a patron saint of the scene. Ken Kesey calls him "Captain Trips." There is also Pigpen, the organist, and Reddy Kilowatt on bass.

Together, the Grateful Dead sound like live thunder. There are no recordings of their music yet, which is probably just as well because no album could duplicate the feeling they generate in a dance hall. I have never seen them live, but I spent an evening at the Fillmore listening to tapes. The music hits hard and stays hard, like early Rolling Stones, but distilled and concentrated. When their new album comes out, I will whip it onto my record player and if they have left that boulder sound at some palatial studio and come out with a polished pebble, I will know they don't live together in the Haight anymore.

But, right now a group called the Grateful Dead is playing live and living for an audience of anybody's kids in San Francisco. Theirs is the Bay Area sound. Nothing convoluted in the lyrics, just rock lingua franca. Not a trace of preciousness in the music; just raunchy funky chords. The big surprise about the San Francisco sound has nothing to do with electronics or some zany new camp. Musicians in this city have knocked all the civility away. They revel in the dark, grainy sound of roots.

"San Francisco is live," says Janis Joplin, of Big Brother and the Holding Company. "Recording in a studio is a completely different trip. No one makes a record like they sound live. Hard rock is the real nitty-gritty."

Ask an aspiring musician from New York who his idols are and he'll begin a long list with the Beatles or Bob Dylan, then branch off into a dozen variations in harmonics and composition.

Not so in San Francisco. Bob Dylan is like Christianity here; they worship but they don't touch. The sound of the Grateful Dead, or Moby Grape, or Country Joe and the Fish, is jug-band music scraping against jazz. This evolution excludes most of the names in modern pop music. A good band is a "heavy" band, a "hard" band.

Marty Balin, who writes for the Jefferson Airplane, declares: "The Beatles are too complex to influence anyone around here. They're a studio sound." Which is as close as a San Francisco

musician comes to describing his thing. Their music, they insist, is a
virgin forest, unchanneled and filled with wildlife. This refusal to
add technological effect is close to the spirit of folk music before
Dylan electrified it. "A rock song still has to have drive and soul,"
Balin maintains. "Jazz started out as dance music, and ended up
dead as something to listen to. If you can't get your effects live,
the music's not alive."

Gary Duncan, lead guitarist for the Quicksilver Messenger
Service, adds: "Playing something in a studio means playing for
two months. Playing live, a song changes in performance. In a
studio, you attack things intellectually; onstage it's all emotion."

San Francisco musicians associate Los Angeles with the evils
of studio music. This is probably because almost every group has
made the trek south to record. And the music available on record
so far is anything but hard rock (the Sopwith Camel, for instance,
earned everyone's disfavor with a lilting good-timey rendition of
"Hello, Hello").

But resentment of Los Angeles goes much deeper than the
recording studio. The rivalry between Northern and Southern California makes a cold war in pop inevitable. While musicians in Los
Angeles deride the sound from up north as "pretentious and self-
conscious" and shudder at the way "people live like animals up
there," the Northern attitude is best summed up by a member of
the Quicksilver Messenger Service who quipped, "L.A. hurts our
eyes."

Part of the Holding Company puts down the Byrds because:
"They had to learn to perform after they recorded. Here, the aim
is to get the crowd moving."

A Jefferson Airplane says of the Beach Boys: "What Brian
Wilson is doing is fine but in person there's no balls. Everything
is pre-fabricated like the rest of that town. Bring them into the
Fillmore, and it just wouldn't work."

The technology involved in putting on a lightshow doesn't seem
to bother San Franciscans, however, because what they're really
uptight about is Southern California. There is a sneaking suspicion
in this city that the South rules and The Bay is determined to keep
at least its cultural supremacy untarnished. Even Ralph Gleason
has little sympathy for Los Angeles music. "The freaks are fostered

and nurtured by L.A. music hype," he says. "The hippies are different. What's going on here is natural and real."

The question of who is commercial and who is authentic is rhetorical. What really matters about San Francisco is what mattered about Liverpool three years ago. The underground occupies a pivotal place in the city's life. The Fillmore and the Avalon are jammed every weekend with beaded, painted faces and flowered shirts. The kids don't come from any mere bohemian quarter. Hip has passed the point where it signifies a commitment to rebellion. It has become *the* style of youth in the Bay Area, just as long hair and beat music were *the* Liverpool Look.

San Francisco is a lot like that grimy English seaport these days. In 1964, Liverpool rang with a sound that was authentically expressive and the city never tried to bury it. This is what is happening in San Francisco today. The establishment has achieved a much greater victory here than on the Strip: integration. The underground is open, unencumbered, and radiating. The rest of the country will get the vibrations, and they will pay for them.

Which everyone thinks is groovy. The Grateful Dead are willing to sing their 20-minute extravaganza, "Midnight Hour," for anyone who will listen, and if people pay, so much the better. But Bob Wier insists: "If the industry is gonna want us, they're gonna take us the way we are. Then, if the money comes in, it'll be a stone gas."

It will be interesting to visit the Bay Area when the breadmen have gutted every artery. It will be fascinating to watch the Fillmore become the Radio City Music Hall of pop music. It will be a stone gas to take a Greyhound sightseeing tour through the Haight.

But that's another story about another San Francisco. Right now, give or take a little corruption, it is new ideas, new faces, and new music.

Which is what undergrounds are all about.

—THE VILLAGE VOICE, 1967

# PETR JANDA: OLYMPIK

PRAGUE—In the late afternoon, they gather above the din of trams and pushcarts, at the top of Prague's main drag—Wenceslas Square. They sit, like ashes on a carpet, where it is most conspicuous, along the steps leading to the National Museum.

They are hippies. Some are students, some give change on street cars, and still others defy the law that requires universal labor or study. They comb their long hair, brush their jeans and cowboy jackets, and chant the pop liturgy as it was constructed in America 10 years ago.

Old people yell "manishka" as they pass. It's an idiom formerly reserved for ugly girls. At the Museum, workers in knit overcoats or billowing overalls stop to ogle. The kids stare back in solidarity. The culture "thaw" in Czechoslovakia has given Prague a taste of the West, but for the "manishkas" it has meant only a melting of ice, making it that much easier to fall through and drown. On the one hand, they can hear music on Radio Luxembourg or Radio Free Europe jam-free. But they cannot buy Western records in the shops. Authorities declare their willingness to sponsor American pop groups, but find the price for most acts prohibitive. And the biggest paradox for hippies is the government's attitude toward their existence. A visitor is informed that Prague is "Modni" enough to sport stylish clothing, and "switched on" enough to tolerate a long-haired youth. But the kids themselves hear little of

120

this bureaucratese. They are too busy running away from the cops, because in Prague, where the elders sneer as they do anywhere, the cops are part-time barbers.

So, when four plainclothesmen close in from either end of the museum, while a police van pulls up the driveway, the kids scatter their playing cards and extinguish their cigarettes. Identity cards are surrendered and inspected.

There are the usual questions about hair and idleness. The unofficial rule requires all males to wear their hair with ears exposed so the more courageous sport pigtails or ponytails. Unsatisfied, the police seize three "manishkas." The next day, the victims return sheepishly to the steps, their hair clipped to bristling crewcuts.

Petr Janda is longhaired and bluejeaned, and he maintains a vicarious contact with the kids on the steps. But he is in no danger of having his bangs clipped because they are a national asset. At 24, he is the lead guitarist and vocalist of Czechoslovakia's top pop group, the Olympiks. Though his face is craggy and his frame stooped, Janda is the one man in Czechoslovakia, and one of the few in the Socialist world, who qualifies as an authentic pop star. He is the *local product*.

The son of a former judge who doubles on the violin in his spare time, Petr studied mechanics, and, after his secondary education, found himself working in Telephone Central as a repairman. After three years of broken circuits and misconnections, he quit to pursue full-time what he had been dabbling in since his school days: rock. He added the magic of electricity to his old guitar by utilizing spare parts. And like countless teens (there are four professional rock groups in Czechoslovakia, but officials estimate that the amateur combos number between 300 and 500), he began to play with friends in small cellar clubs. He signed with the Sputniks who, in 1959, became the first pop group to be licensed by the Cultural Bureau. When the Sputniks split three years ago, Janda joined the newly forming Olympiks. The group thrived and has since recorded more than 30 songs. Their biggest hit, "Give Me More of Your Love," sold 40,000 discs—a smash by Czech standards.

Today, the Olympiks play nightly in their own club. Fans sit politely at long formica tables, trying to ignore the wood paneling and dour paintings which adorn the walls. There is smoking and

clapping but no screaming in the audience. The pop magic does not apply to the Olympiks because they are as familiar as the streetcars. Petr Janda can walk down the street with his clothing intact and his features unpummeled. His fans are loyal, but unecstatic.

"All young people in Czechoslovakia are for American culture," he says. The Olympiks try to fill that need, though vicariously. They wear a uniform of bluejeans and black turtleneck sweaters. Their repertory includes some original songs and some made famous by groups like the Stones, the Kinks, and the Animals. But they always sing in English. When Petr speaks English, his voice shakes as he grasps for equivalents, but he sings in a strong baritone:

> I sleep through the day
> I wake around four
> But I always feel down
> Never get off the floor

Hardly the Socialist vision; hardly an image of smiling workers in a field of waving corn, their feet and hands swaying in a dance of progress. This is the Czechoslovakia you see on the back of coins. But Petr Janda says: "The Olympiks do not like the worker mentality." The four musicians who play with him snicker at his reference. "The workers are stupid," says Ladislav Klien, the rhythm guitarist. "They accept without questioning. They see you walk down the street, and they come up to touch your hair. They are laughing at your clothes or your girlfriend. Young people are very little fans for the Communists."

Pop musicians everywhere are usually reluctant to talk politics with foreigners, but the Olympiks, perhaps because they are young and popular, are quite willing to voice their dissatisfaction. In Czechoslovakia, as throughout Eastern Europe, the government has undergone a discernible change in its attitude toward pop. Articles written during the late '50s decried this "revisionism from the West." But the pop boycott did little to loosen its hold, and in the early sixties an official policy of peaceful co-existence prevailed. Twist lessons were given in Czech schools, and Elvis Presley —never enthusiastically greeted by the government—was at least acknowledged in print.

Today the government, through local culture centers, youth magazines, and the national record company, Supraphon, has stepped into the pop business with a vengeance. Its aim seems to be the production of groups to rival those in the West. Radio Prague plays pop—East and West—every afternoon. Concerts to determine which groups should receive professional status are held annually here, as they are in Poland and Hungary.

The Olympiks happen to be the foremost expression of the Czech pop style. Though they are not immune to government censure, they are not exactly threatened by it either. Jan Anthpacak, the drummer, notes: "We are not popular in the high offices," but though all rock groups must play before a culture commission twice a year to renew their licenses, the Olympiks have never encountered any trouble. They are the only group in Czechoslovakia who travel abroad. Of all combos, the Olympiks have least to complain about. Karel Svoboda, who writes and sings for the Mefisto, another leading group, says he receives 60 crowns (16 to the dollar) for a disc, and 125 for a performance. One percent of the profits on a record goes to the artists and writers. Ninety-nine percent goes to the state. The Olympiks are better paid, but even they are aware that their equivalents in other countries are worshipped, not only by the fans, but by the banks.

Now the group swings seriously into rehearsal, while, from the balcony, a cleaning woman and repairman watch in stunned disbelief. Once onstage, the Olympiks undergo an electronic transformation. Their accents and mannerisms fade into the music. When they sing "Help," they are the Beatles. When they jump into "Sunny Afternoon," they become the Kinks. It is only during the breaks, when Ladislav screams about the quality of percussion or vocal, that the musicians become, again, kids from Prague. Ladislav is the fanatic of the group. "When I was a student," he says, "my father didn't let me hear music. So naturally, I learned to play it. Now, the money is good."

Petr Janda agrees. The money is good. He dresses himself and his 21-year-old fiancee, Jana, in the latest Czech mod gear. When she comes to the club, she wears a pea coat, jersey pullover, and tweed skirt. She usually brings—along with her broad grin—a few bottles of Czech beer (very good) or Czech cola (awful) for the

boys. Jana has a few questions for any American she meets: What is a Lovin' Spoonful? When will we end the war in Vietnam? What does Coca-Cola taste like? There are still cities in the world where words like "New York" open eyes wide, and Prague is one of those places. But the Olympiks see and sing America through a glass, very darkly.

—THE VILLAGE VOICE, 1967

# THE INSULATED HIPPIE AWAKENS

TORONTO, Ontario—Yorkville Avenue ambles past three sanitized blocks of frame houses turned boutiques. Shade trees shelter a generous sidewalk from sunny glare, so no one really needs shades. The street is ideal for ogling. On Friday and Saturday nights, all of Talc Toronto and his date are there, getting a weekend scene-tan. Their eyes are cemented to rows of neat black guard-rails which line the street. Around these hitching posts, hippies sprawl, rap, and ogle back.

It is a hippy Disneyland, in plastic tribute to last month's Time-style on the Now Generation. For in Yorkville, though the hucksters hustle, the tourists hassle, and the cops harass, it all seems premeditated like a carnival. The hippies provide a handy freak show, but they are insulated from real degenerates and junkies. Unlike the Haight-Ashbury or the East Village, Yorkville is a high-rent district, filled with quaint cottages and high-rise formica. Many of the hippies who inhabit the area (a minority of those who actually make the scene) live five and six to a luxury room. It is a crowded life, but fairly clean. Even the air is remarkably reekless for a hippie neighborhood. Everyone talks about turning on, but you don't see much of it, and it isn't easy to come by.

Finally, as if it were not hard enough to drop out along the strip without landing in mosquito net, Yorkville is curse-blessed with a coterie of indulgent journalists who measure social phe-

nomena by the column-inch. Hippies express themselves on a wide variety of issues, certain they will read about it in the morning papers. What else is there in Toronto to frighten the gentry, with wars and riots happening elsewhere?

On a good night flashbulbs pop like strobelights. With media weaving among the teenyboppers, Yorkville has produced its own corps of celebrities. Robert Gilgour, a 67-year-old pensioner, is known on every city desk as "a friend to all hippies." He keeps a freezer full of sandwiches for hungry kids (though not many starve on Yorkville Avenue, with home often a suburb away) and inspires a small band of followers who call themselves '49ers.

Then there are the leather angels. In Toronto they are the Vagabonds, and they sputter about on their California-style choppers. That is, occasionally. More often, you see them in small bands, colors hanging limply around their shoulders rapping with the street hippies who worshipfully announce the presence of a "Vag" in the vicinity.

If they aren't around, a rock star or a draft dodger can make a tourist's evening out. Yorkville is thought to be filled with both. For musicians, stardom comes with a New York engagement. The logo "just back from New York" is ubiquitous as a minimum in Toronto's rock cellars. But the most mystical fixtures—the Paupers, the Mandala, the Kensington Market, or Luke and the Apostles— are not to be seen in Yorkville on summer nights. Recording and travel-gigs come first and, as for leisure, the street is just too gross for a superstar.

Draft dodgers, on the other hand, are easy enough to come by in Yorkville, but difficult to authenticate. Actually, most Americans avoid the hip scene because of the ease with which they can be deported. But groupies flock to any stranger who announces his exile. It is only when the immigrant reveals his real home town (Saskatoon) in a moment of weakness that the shoulders shrug, the brows bristle in annoyance, and the back turns utterly.

But the teenyboppers are not the only ones who think Yorkville is swollen with draft dodgers. The gray populace sees the hip community as augmented and inspired by unwashed, unrepentant, un-Canadian youth. Widely-published reports negate this theory, but it persists. Mothers and ministers have suggested that the

hippies be driven across the border (preferably over Niagara Falls) where they will be drafted instantly. The concept of the U.S. as a ranting Big Daddy with spurs has led to the conclusion in Canada that all hippies anywhere are really Americans in disguise.

After all—hippies in Toronto? Flower children germinating among the neat cottages and Eskimo art shops? Gurus in a city where the French and Indians know their place? The Love Generation commuting to its appointed rounds on North America's cleanest subway system?

Marshall McLuhan must have brought them, the way a filthy neighbor brings roaches, and he can take them back to New York with him, where they belong.

Not a few of Toronto's gentry blame their city's philosopher-king for the hip incursion. McLuhan is more highly regarded than heeded here, and he is only incidentally an influence on the cultural mores of Toronto. Media-gazing will never replace ice hockey.

Still, McLuhan's tenure has given this town a heady whiff of big-city chic. To the literati, hippies are its fruition (these days it takes a rebellious youth, not a skyline, to make a city). But to the sofa-squatters, they are its unwanted legacy. And Toronto is a Midwestern matron, rising on the great lakes in mini-majesty. She sips her avant-garde in small, sweet doses like a cocktail. Getting stoned is not allowed.

She stood leaning against a guard-rail, surveying the strip. Mary Kerson, the Digger from New York (touch her). A veteran of all the great wars—from Tompkins Square to Steve Paul's Scene—she had come to Toronto to help the local Diggers incorporate. There was to be a fully-licensed hostel for indigent hippies, a food-distribution center, a medical clinic, and possibly a newspaper. To feed Yorkville's corporate head, the visitor produced $5000 from the New York brethren, and a promise of more.

It made the papers. The kids on the strip buzzed with excitement, like *braceros* straining to hear the word "huelga." Even the Village Bar Association (two young lawyers-in-training who man a table on the street to check on civil liberties violations from the kids) noticed the change. Their clients weren't whimpering about illegal

search and seizure anymore. They were boning up on penalties for civil disobedience.

The clarion call came from a small mascot called "Dog." One tourist-ridden night he was pushed from the jammed sidewalk into the path of the cruising caravan. Dog's death brought a long-standing grievance to the fore. The kids wanted their street closed to traffic. What they were really demanding was an end to the tourist trade, and at that prospect the owners of Yorkville balked.

So when a small hippie band danced around a bonfire in the middle of Yorkville Avenue, six were arrested. That night 350 of their friends sat in the street. With 3000 onlookers whooping it up and traffic stalled for blocks, they had finally broken the rules.

The vans pulled up slowly. A force of tactical police set about cleaning up the demonstrators, while reinforcements detoured traffic onto Yorkville Avenue, so that the flow would be especially heavy. The hippies linked arms, giggling, chanting, and displaying profiles of their tongues for the press. They couldn't be pulled apart. But as bulbs flashed, traffic shrieked, and tourists jeered, the police came apart instead. Aided by squads of plainclothesmen, they waded into the jangling squatters, and slammed away. It was what the underground press calls a "police riot" and it seemed as though the ground rules had been laid on Sunset Strip. Screaming hippies were clubbed and pummeled before they could move. Ribs cracked, blood flowed, hair came loose. A demonstrator was hurled head-first into a waiting van. One girl, her hand smashed under a policeman's foot, narrowly avoided having it amputated. And, as the crowd threatened to join in, a phalanx of policemen dragged the friend of all hippies—Robert Gilgour—off to jail.

That was too much. As the presses rolled, the people of Toronto learned over morning coffee that their finest had brutalized a peaceful demonstration. "Police Beat Up Hippies" screamed the Globe and Mail; "52 Jailed for Sitting in Street," boomed the Telegram: "More Trouble Feared." And the Toronto Star editorialized: "No excuse for police brutality."

Amid an embarrassed insistence by the police that only necessary force was used ("These reporters," scowled a police deskman. "In some cities, they're hard on hoods. Here, it's us"), the hippies held another sit-in, this one in the gray corridors of the old City Hall.

Clerks and cops watched in stunned silence as the kids cheered whenever a prisoner was released. A stout, smiling photographer asked injured hippies to hold up their bandages for display. Necktie tucked neatly into his pants, he snapped, and beamed, and snapped again. When Gilgour was released, waving limply, the photographer nearly split his cheeks with delight.

"Hold it; hold it, pops."

He did.

When Dave De Poe joined the Company of Young Canadians (roughly equivalent to VISTA) at 23, he chose to take up residence in Yorkville. He rented a house off the strip, went about making friends, and started the Diggers. De Poe's father, a well-known TV commentator, disapproved. The tension between them made De Poe a natural celebrity in Yorkville, but his talent for organization made him a useful one. He walked the streets like everyone's favorite worker-priest, in a flat-brimmed hat, beard and moustache. You almost expected the kids to kiss his ring and call him "father." But De Poe studiously avoided the hip mystique some Diggers solicit. With assistants like Brian (Blues) Chapman he built a tight yet casual net around the strip, catching in the rye.

To Downtown Toronto, De Poe was an agitator—the cause, not the mitigator, of hip lawlessness. When the riots came, he was down in the street, and the police tagged him instantly as a ringleader. Only his position with the CYC kept De Poe from becoming the brunt of their frustration. As one officer raised his fist, another intervened with the riot line of the year: "Not him, for heaven sake. He works for the federal government."

De Poe's supervisor, Alan Clarke, reported that exchange from his desk in Ottawa where he had been asked by reporters to defend his employe against charges of agitation. Clarke said De Poe's involvement in the scene had actually been "beneficial in Yorkville." He told a reporter: "As far as we're concerned, he is where we want him to be."

On the afternoon following his second arrest, De Poe sat in his living room, welcoming visitors from one of Canada's larger television stations. The director chatted softly about his "project."

"We're doing this hippie thing, Davey. And what we plan is,

we'll pick you up tomorrow, and take you out to—oh, somewhere in the suburbs, and just ask you what you think of it. You know, just stand there and tell us what you think."

De Poe, who had not slept in two days, nodded lamely, as two cameramen and a lady reporter in high tweed arrived to set up. "Let's get some of these posters in," she chortled. "Who is this one—Mao?"

"Ho." De Poe muttered, lacing up a sneaker.

"Oh don't do that just yet. Can you . . . er . . . take your shirt off and we'll just catch you putting it on? Don't put your socks on yet . . . Oh, you're not going to wear socks. Oh, and . . . you're . . . uh . . . your underwear is, um, sticking out in front."

Cameras finally rolling, De Poe began his lecture. "What the pickets in the street mean is 'We'd like to talk to the people of Toronto. We want to ask the Mayor about closing our street.' But the Mayor is uptight."

Blues raced up the stairs and burst into view before the camera. "Cops are already gathering in the park," he puffed. "They're in plain clothes all over the Village."

The camera clicked shut. The reporter stepped forward, fingering a tiny rhinestone earring. "Would you say that again? We can . . . um . . . use that to set up for what's going to happen later . . . uh, potentially, of course."

Yorkville Avenue at dusk looked like an encampment three hours after retreat. Slings and bandages decorated in art-nouveau were everywhere. Scabs blossomed on upper lips. Newspapers covered the sidewalks as tight clusters of hippies read about themselves and their opponents. The arch-villain was controller Alan Lamport, who demanded that hippies be banished from Yorkville for a full year. "Some of them think they can get anything their sweet heart desires," he told the Toronto *Star*. "They have a spoiled brat attitude."

Dave De Poe left his house, cameramen and reporters trailing behind. Down the street, a kid with matted hair raced into an alley pursued by a stout, crewcut plainclothesman. De Poe darted away while Blues distracted the TV crew with an imaginary scuffle up ahead.

When they found him five minutes later, De Poe was heading the line of march toward Queens Park. Waving placards and incense, they made their way down treelined streets, while dinnertime strollers gaped. Churchbells rang in the distance, and ministers from a nearby seminary stopped dead in their tracks. "Take our blood in hospitals; not in the streets," read one placard. A cabdriver snarled at the procession, and two ladies giggled.

On hippie hill the '49ers distributed oranges and peanut-butter sandwiches. Members of the Village Bar collected complaints of police brutality, preparing for a massive civilian suit. Then, with no chanting of "Hare Krishna" (that litany hasn't arrived here yet), the meeting got underway.

De Poe counseled moderation, but avoided a firm stand. From the sidelines, his father watched sullenly. It was the first time he had seen his son in action. Later, the two met briefly, and parted with their backs turned.

As lampposts flickered on across Toronto, the hippies returned to their strip. Already, Yorkville Avenue was jammed beyond recognition with bystanders searching in vain for the real hippies. When they arrived, the police—in a far more sober mood after the morning papers—edged away from the sidewalks and waited.

But no one sat in the street that night. When a cluster of hippies fell on their knees on the sidewalk, the police moved gingerly, forcing them to stand, but not rushing them. Their orders were encased in words like "please" and "sir." Only eight arrests were made all evening, and the crowds grew restless. They tried to goad the police into action. Shorthaired kids from the suburbs vowed to act on their own if the hippies couldn't. When the police moved in on horses to control the onlookers, snapping flashbulbs and flicked cigarettes sent the animals scurrying down the street, to cheers and whistles. The hippies found themselves outflanked by juicers; nearly half the arrests involved drunkenness.

It was a tense scene. So, the word spread through the hippies' ranks: split. They moved silently back to the park, leaving the police to face a concentrated version of Yorkville on any Saturday night.

Queens Park was midnight-still when the hippies arrived. They sat silently around their hill, as Dave De Poe told them he had to

leave for an appearance on a late-night TV talk show. He parted with the words: "we're winning."

And they were. In three days, they had shattered their own insulation and made a sterile stretch of plastic bohemia something worth fighting over. In Montreal and Vancouver, kids were picking up their morning papers and marveling. Maybe next year at this time, the hippies will be stopping traffic on Yorkville Avenue with uprooted trees. Maybe Dave De Poe and Blues will collect money to send their friends to Europe. Or maybe they will mix with the beautiful people and go the penthouse route.

But it will be a while before Toronto society makes the Yorkville hippies an in-crowd and perhaps they won't accept that title when it comes. They looked far better sitting in Queens Park eating oranges as a big-sister Digger from New York told them: "We're a movement now, and we've got to sound like one."

Everyone agreed—they should sing "We Shall Overcome" but nobody knew the words. So Mary Kerson from the East Village led them, line by line, and they sang softly as red embers from cruising squad cars singed the trees above.

—THE VILLAGE VOICE, 1967

# C. J. FISH ON SATURDAY

It was Saturday afternoon and the Algonquin Hotel smelled of old marble and mahogany. In his suite, Country Joe MacDonald sat on a sofa and watched cartoons on color TV. They were strange, frenzied fantasies filled with ultraviolet dragons and heroic white whales. Aggression was the dominant theme and the plots amounted to a series of battles, with flashes of color the only sign of impact. Joe watched for twenty minutes, holding a wind-up policeman doll in his hand. You turn the key and the head bobs and the club moves up and down.

I was there to rap about the revolution. Since the Fish have come to represent the quintessence of commitment in a rock group, I was searching for a few predictions, a reminiscence of life at the barricades, and perhaps a scenario or two. But Country Joe snickered. "There isn't going to be any revolution. Let's be realistic," and he went off to brush his teeth.

Barry Melton, who plays guitar and has hair like a liberated sheep, took up the TV watch. I asked him about Chicago, anticipating a barage of quotable dialectic.

"Well, we were walking into this hotel and these guys with armbands came by. They followed us into the lobby and attacked us." End of manifesto.

Country Joe returned wearing a brocade vest and a straw hat. He picked up the toy cop again, while Barry called room service

133

for breakfast. "We've got a photo session—this afternoon—3:30, I think."

"Why isn't there going to be a revolution?"

"Because you have to control things, and most of the people I know aren't ready for that. They want a leaderless society."

"What about the guerillas?" I offered.

"I don't know any. I know a lot of people wearing Che Guevara teeshirts . . . what a bunch of tripped-out freaks. Three years ago, we were hobos, singing our hearts out about the virtues of the open road. Last year, we were Indians. Now we're revolutionaries. Man, if the revolution ever comes for real, they'll probably use Andy Warhol munitions. You throw it and this big sign comes on—'Pow.' "

He sank back into the sofa. His wife and their new baby were back in California, and they had left him with the puffy look of someone rendered incomplete. But his apathy was more than the result of separation. What you call "the vibes" when you want to give a hip name to the transference of energy is gone. You don't notice it on their new album right away, but live, that sharp certainty has given way to something almost laconic. The Fish still push the same old stuff, but the high is different now. Melodies are shattered, lyrics barely coherent. Oh, the language is stronger (the old Fish cheer now reads, "Gimme an F . . . U . . . C . . . etc" and "that bastard LBJ" has become "that motherfucker") but the sound is disjointed, dazed. Only the symptoms of energy remain. Joe stands limply through most of the set, the swing gone from his body, the muscle in his head rarely flexed.

I asked him why his music had changed. He straightened up slowly and took off his hat. "See, we're not what we thought we were."

"How so?"

"Well, two years ago, we believed in music like a god. If you're gonna get into a heavy acid trip, you're gonna get religious. If you stop taking acid, you stop being religious."

"Our audience knew we got stoned and we knew they got stoned and it all worked in a big circle," Barry added.

"Yeah, but music's nothing to believe in. I mean, it's just sound."

"Do you feel like quitting now?"

"No, I still dig playing. If it got really bad, I couldn't even get

up on the stage. But today, the only emotion I associate with music is pleasure. There used to be all kinds of . . . well . . . connotations."

In the distance we heard a shout that sounded like "Dump the Hump," so we ran to the window and raised the blinds. It was a small march to Times Square, complete with Vietcong flags and a police escort. From the hotel, we could see only a sliver of it. Joe smiled, drew the blinds, and turned the volume up on the TV.

"This is C. J. Fish," Barry was grumbling into the phone. "We didn't get any coffee with that food."

"It's hard to sing for real anymore," Joe said, sinking back onto the couch. "Our music is all noise . . . protest noise."

The bell rang and an old acquaintance offered greetings and news from the barricades. Heavy guerilla scenes in the East Village; Columbia was perking and almost ready to pour again. By the way, could the group make a benefit?

Joe said no, they'd be back in California with their families, and the kid wondered why the Fish weren't doing so many street gigs anymore. Barry explained that the music doesn't work in a charged street situation, because the equipment is expensive and immobile. If the cops come you can't split with an amp on your back.

The talk turned to politics. "The revolution is just another word for working within the community," the friend incanted.

"Yeah, but I'm not into that anymore," Joe said.

"What are you into?"

"Robin and the kid . . . and me."

"But Joe, other kids are in the streets, and they're gonna be laying down a whole new thing."

"I don't believe in the revolution."

"Hell, you *are* the revolution, so how could you not believe in it?"

"Because there is no revolution. I'm just living out my lifestyle. That's what you should be doing."

"Obviously we're using the word differently."

"Look, you want to be a revolutionary? It means time—ten, fifteen years—so go back to school. Become a revolutionary in school."

"Why don't you go back to school?"

"Because I've got a career as a poet, an entertainer, and a musician."

"Yeah, well maybe my career is listening to you. And maybe I have to fight to do that."

"Bullshit. You're no revolutionary. You're just a young American citizen in the twentieth century."

"No I'm not."

"Aha, took away your identity."

The hostility is getting a bit thick, so Barry suggests they split for the photographer's studio. Everyone stands and Joe shoves the hat down over his eyes. "I've been a poet, a guru, a politico," he says. "I'll be anything you want. Tell me what you want me to be."

Nobody answers. "Well, I'm in the entertainment business right now. It just so happens that the people I entertain are freaky."

In the lobby there are no groupies or agents, and just a couple of honeymooners at a registration desk. Barry grabs a cab and jumps in. "Whyanchacutyerhair?" the driver snarls, and I shake hands with Joe and walk away. At home, I open my notebook to search for a closing line. I find it tucked under a hammer and sickle doodle.

Country Joe MacDonald is half Jewish.

—THE VILLAGE VOICE, 1968

# ● KICK OUT THE JAMS

Detroit may have gone for Humphrey, but it's Nixon country—a vast, gray flatbed gone dour with the resignation of an industrial spa. The streets are straight, the houses frame, and the people—well, the best one can say is that they form a city of rank and file. It's hard to guess whether the giant tire which hovers over the airport expressway is someone's idea of an L.A. joke, or an authentic religious symbol. At very least, that plaster imitation of a rubber wheel is the totem of Detroit.

I had come to see the MC 5. Three things intrigued me about this band. First, they were the only group to play Lincoln Park during the Democratic convention. For a group with no capital to risk its equipment, not to mention its lives, takes a special kind of commitment bordering on joy. Yet the risk had been worthwhile, even commercially. The MC 5 are already known in pop-critical circles (in which I mean to include everyone who has never published in *The New York Review of Books*) as an authentic guerilla-rock band, which encourages screwing and smoking, and are not even averse to livening up a slow set by shitting onstage.

They live in Ann Arbor, a college town thirty minutes out of Detroit. It's peaceful here—mostly, I suspect, because the violence is regimented around the taking of exams. There are trees and sky, and that crisp Midwestern smell, like a young girl's cheek. If you have a tribe, Ann Arbor seems a far more reasonable place to

137

stake out turf than, say, the Lower East Side. For one thing, it's spacious, and for another, there are plenty of townies to offer tea and sympathy to a resident freak.

The MC 5 and their people share a rambling twenty room house near the University of Michigan campus. The floors are clean, the stereo system is in good condition, and the dope facilities are excellent. In the basement, their manager John Sinclair runs the commune known as Trans-Love Energies, edits a local broadside called *The Sun,* devises propaganda for the "White Panther Party," publishes local poets, and organizes artists' workshops. As a veteran beatnik and jazz-freak, Sinclair has infused the entire group with his scene. That enlightenment covers the MC 5 like cheap polish. Just underneath the surface, you can feel the real grain, and it's rough. Run your hands over the MC 5, and you get splinters.

They've been playing together in the Detroit area for four years, building a local following for their spasm-rock. It's been a lean time for raunch, what with the jazz-folk-raga blend in vogue. You couldn't picture the MC 5 playing before an audience of 20,000 stoned love children—not with the fire and brimstone in their sound. No wonder they hate all ornate music, as well as the light and flower cosmology that goes with it. The whole hip circus is what kept them down.

Today, they are fiercely proud of the elements of angry black jazz in their music. It is not the passive saintliness of blues they worship, or the stylized exuberance of soul. They're after demonsound—noise for conjuring—, searing, and pressing honkies everywhere up against a wall (any wall will do). Their allusions are all within the R and B genre, but ironically, it is the white-boy rock 'n' roller jive that stays with you after the tonal assault has died down.

Dissecting their music into riffs and fills, you sense an immense void in the area I can only call literacy. We have been conditioned to accept experimentation in the guise of primitive music. The primacy of the recording studio, coupled with an abundance of stereo home equipment, has resulted in a compartmentalization of the rock experience. Today's solos—even when they are improvised —sound diagrammed, as though the ebb and flow of energy were being fed through channels.

But the MC 5 come on live and whole. They move with the kind of energy long gone from rock, but not forgotten. Up onstage, they do the Chuck Berry cakewalk, the Little Richard split, the James Brown kneedrop, the Jackie Wilson leap. There is only one other rock group which utilizes these cliches with such mastery of the logistics of rock: the Who. The similarities between Pete Townshend and the MC 5's guitarist, Wayne Kramer, suggests that they both draw their energy from the same roots. And both perform with a reverence which is the most authentic kind of commitment a musician can display. That's what makes a band and a scene.

In Detroit, the scene is centered around the Grande Ballroom, a dancehall done up in Midwestern Mooresque. The surrounding streets are still gutted with riot-ruins (empty lots filled with splintered brick and glass). Speeding by in a car, the neighborhood looks like the inside of a six-year-old's mouth, with gaps where the baby teeth should be. But inside, it's wall-to-wall rapport. For its solidarity alone, Detroit reminds me of Greenwich Village in 1963, Liverpool in 1965, San Francisco in 1967. In all these places, you could tell a music scene was authentic by the influence it extended over people's style.

The MC 5 do that much for Detroit. When Brother J. C. gives his White Panther pitch, hands go up in eager fists. Flags are burned on the spot. Chairs and mikes are smashed. Like in the old days.

Outside the Grande tonight, Elektra Records has set up a portable studio in the belly of a rented truck. All the tumult onstage is compressed onto those everpresent spools of tape. But there is something symbolic in the subservience of this studio; it represents an astute recognition that the MC 5—if they are to matter at all—must matter live. All the mixing and mastering in Christendom won't improve their sound as much as an audience shrieking whenever the lead singer commands: "Kick out the jams, motherfuckers!"

The kids get the point (and the MC 5 is definitely a kid's group). Far from the random ecstasy of a California freak-out, theirs is a highly directed release of energy. These are the children of insurgency; no wonder they expect their culture to coerce. To watch them standing under the strobes, hands raised in youth-salute, is

to understand how pop art can serve as a political mirror, refracting reality through slogan and myth. Undeniably, there is fascism in the MC 5 and the ecstasy they provide. Not just because they make you want to kill the foreigners (in this case, adults), but because they suggest the terrible relationship between right and might which is at the core of all art.

At home, after the Grande gig, there is music and dope and spaghetti cooking in the kitchen. Girls scurry about, brewing tea, changing records, making conversation. A neighbor arrives with two gift pumpkins. And the group sits around an immense dining room table, rubbing their bellies and pounding their forks. They put my head into Huns. Warriors. The conqueror race. I tell Wayne his music is very violent, because that's all I can think of to describe fifteen minutes of sheer volume punctuated by the stab of a strobe light. Violent. He gives a soft, certain smile, and answers: "Well, that's rock 'n' roll."

—THE VILLAGE VOICE, 1968

# ● LOVE: A GROOVY IDEA WHILE HE LASTED

We are all victims of symbols. Events breed their own ritual. Maybe that is why the murders of James Leroy Hutchinson and Linda Fitzpatrick read like Act Three of an off-off-Broadway play. The truest theatre of the '60's lies spiked across the city desk, slugged "slay."

What happened at 169 Avenue B happens all the time. A man and his woman are hauled or lured down to the boiler room, where amid rags and ratsmell she is banged senseless, and both are stomped dead.

Such crimes become incidents. We never hear about them unless the woman was pregnant, mutilated, or both. But Groovy and his girl were slaughtered right on page one of the *Daily News*. Journalists made pilgrimages to Tompkins Square and its adjoining shrines. Even Mayor Lindsay took note. When he called the murders "a tragedy" he was speaking not about the crime but its particulars. The tragedy in what went down on Avenue B is who went down, and who did the felling.

Some crimes seem to apotheosize an age. This time, only the corpses make it improper to write off victims and villains as an allegory staged by some playwright-deity. We would have waited in line to see it in the theatre, specifying alternate dates and all the rest, while on a stage set as a boiler room masked hippies and black militants dance a stylized ballet, feigning death and delight.

141

In quite Phil Ochs voices, we would inquire of the stagehands: "Have you got a picture of the pain?"

Photos were plentiful. "His own weird world turned against him," crooned the *Daily News*. In centerfold obituaries they immortalized Groovy as a speed-saint, guru-clown, lover-dealer. Crucified by gangster-Romans, he became a true martyr. As a reformer of meth swindlers, his arrest for possession of a deadly weapon seemed irrelevant. How well he personified the love ethic, and how much more perfect he was as a symbol than he must have been as a man!

He and his girl were buried last week in their respective cultures. Linda's velvet-draped casket was carried down an Episcopal aisle while the minister chanted from the Book of Common Prayer. She rode to her burial in a gray Cadillac. Groovy's funeral was conducted in a Baptist minister's parlor. As a eulogy, Galahad played the harmonica that was part of his friend's costume.

Neither coffin was arrayed with flowers, which was appropriate. Both were victims of such symbols. They were beautiful people, and beautiful victims. They followed their alleged assailants into the basement, exuding love and groove. And they died near a pile of their clothing, not merely rubbed out, but smashed faceless.

The *News* eulogized Linda Fitzpatrick as "a pretty fair-skinned aspiring artist who clung to the fringes of hippiedom, terrified of the denizens of the accursed land, but fascinated by them." Gone are Linda's beads and bangles; the papers were filled with straight rich-girl snapshots. She too lost her personality in allegory. Her swirling stares and speed-chatter were buried in a reserved coffin. To the *News* and its audience, she was not high but afraid.

That fear is all over the East Village today. The murders were too plausible to be ignored, the suspects too real to be dismissed. No one escapes the media, including its antagonists. Everyone knows that Groovy died in a mandala of his own blood. And suddenly, everyone remembers why. Other killings come to mind; not the publicized ones—like the fatal stabbing of Walter Coey on his stoop on East 11th, or the bizarre ones—like the Central Park mugging of Bruce Mantel, "the poet," and the rape of his 15-year-old "flower bride." They remember the casual murders (five or six since the early summer, some claim). Accounts of unreported

rape abound, and hallway muggings seem to be a rite-de-passage east of Tompkins Square.

It is a slum; Groovy's death seems to have awakened that realization. And hippies, they mutter, are the new niggers. "The odds are incredibly stacked," they say. "There is opposition from every corner." "Flower power was a summer vacation," they hiss. "In San Francisco, they staged the death of the hippie. Here, we got the real thing."

The mindblower is not that love is dead in the East Village, but that it has taken this long to kick the bucket. Flower power began and ended as a cruel joke. The last laugh belongs to the mediamen, who chose to report a charade as a movement. In doing so, they created one. By the thousands, the real victims of flower hype poured into the slums of both coasts. *Life-Look* filled its pages with technicolor testimonials to the young drop-outs living the love ethic their leaders were wary of. There was a bizarre camaraderie between the fourth estate and the fifth dimension. Aspiring scene-makers quickly mastered the art of journalistic posturing; one facade, they discovered, was better than a thousand words. Every daily paper picked its own hippie spokesman. The *Post* latched onto Abbie Hoffman, and in their tradition of prophetic misprints, called him a "Bigger" and his followers "Happies." The *Times* found Galahad and made him the East Village Lawrence of Arabia. Reluctant, willing, or both, these men too became symbols and hired killers. They found they could mainline their pronouncements into the American bloodstream through the press. The price they paid for being culture definers was their sacred anonymity. Those who accepted the new definition became its ultimate victims.

The flower children, high on love, brought their material feast to areas of constant famine, and then went on a hunger strike. Even in rags, they seemed wealthy. Even destitute, they knew their rights and privileges. The attention they won from the press, and the police, made reprisals inevitable. "The hippies really bug us," a young black East Sider told the *Times*. "Because we know they can come down here and play their games for awhile and then escape. And we can't, man."

Only now, after Groovy's murder, is there talk about madness

of counseling large-scale settlement of the ghetto by drop-outs from the middle class. Only now are flower children wondering why anyone woud sleep in Central Park, or offer flowers to a raging madman. And only as the Summer of Love chills into a violent harvest is there talk of getting out. Like generations of Lower East Siders before them, the Group Image wants to move to the country. Abbie Hoffman wants to split for San Francisco. In supermarkets and psychedelic shops, a rash of neatly printed notices has appeared, offering cash and gratitude for the return of a son or daughter. The old folks are scared, but so are the kids. Those who cannot change may claim their own rewards.

Groovy's legacy is a new slum-hippie. He lives in the ghetto, and he acts like it. He sees his scene for what it is. "The mystique has worn off," he says. "People are beginning to admit the ugliness of it now. The myths are peeling away, like bad paint, man. Take the drug thing. This is an amphetamine scene here. Part of your flower power survival kit is meth. It's ugly, and it's real, man. And it was here all along, for anyone to see who felt like it."

The new hippie is on the scene already, even as the media-ministers whisper "dust to dust, ashes to ashes" over his saint of an ancestor. Galahad helped usher him in when he told the *Daily News,* "Just give me ten minutes alone with whoever did this to my friend Groovy." The word has gotten around that some Diggers in New York and San Francisco carry guns—and intend to use them. The flower child, now a veteran of violence, is toughening up. Did we expect anything else? For a long time now we have been glibly informed that the most logical way to cope with the culture of poverty is psychosis. Dare we demand sanity from the slum-hippie?

"I respect those who respect me," he says, with a passing glance at the east side of Tompkins Square Park. You ask about the mood on the streets and he smiles. From beneath his corduroy robes he produces a wooden shaft painted in dayglo swirls. It snaps open to reveal an erect steel blade.

"Love," he mutters, "was a Groovy idea—while he lasted."

—THE VILLAGE VOICE, 1967

# IV
# SOUNDS

# I BLEW MY COOL THROUGH THE NEW YORK TIMES

The Beatles spent an unprecedented four months and $100,000 on their new album, *Sergeant Pepper's Lonely Hearts Club Band*. Like fathers-to-be, they kept a close watch on each stage of its gestation. For they are no longer merely superstars. Hailed as progenitors of a pop avant-garde, they have been idolized as the most creative members of their generation. The pressure to create an album that is complex, profound, and innovative must have been staggering. So they retired to the electric sanctity of their recording studio, dispensing with their adoring audience and the shrieking inspiration it can provide.

The finished product reached the record racks last week; the Beatles had supervised even the album cover—a mind-blowing collage of famous and obscure people, plants, and artifacts. The 12 new compositions in the album are as elaborately conceived as the cover. The sound is a pastiche of dissonance and lushness. The mood is mellow, even nostalgic. But, like the cover, the over-all effect is busy, hip, and cluttered.

If being a critic were the same as being a listener, I could enjoy *Sergeant Pepper's Lonely Hearts Club Band*. Other than one song which I detest ("Good Morning, Good Morning"), I find the album better than 80 percent of the music around today. But it is the other 20 percent—including the best of the Beatles' past performances—which worries me, as a critic.

147

When the Beatles' work as a whole is viewed in retrospect, *Rubber Soul* and *Revolver* will stand as their major contributions. When the slicks and tricks of production on this new album no longer seem unusual, and the compositions are stripped to their musical and lyrical essentials, *Sergeant Pepper* will be Beatles baroque—an elaboration without improvement.

Like an over-attended child, this album is spoiled. It reeks of horns and harps, harmonica quartets, assorted animal noises, and a 41-piece orchestra. Sometimes, this elaborate musical propwork succeeds in projecting mood. The "Sergeant Pepper" theme is brassy and vaudevillian. "Lucy In The Sky With Diamonds" is scored with stinging dissonance, and "She's Leaving Home" is drenched in maraschino strings. In what is becoming a Beatles tradition, George Harrison unveils his latest excursion into curry and karma, to the saucy accompaniment of three tamburas, a dilruba, a tabla, a sitar, a table harp, three cellos, and eight violins.

Harrison's song, "Within You and Without You," is a good place to begin dissecting *Sergeant Pepper*. Though it is among the album's stronger cuts, its flaws are distressingly typical of the work as a whole. Harrison's voice—hovering midway between song and prayer chant—oozes over the melody like melted cheese. Because his raga motifs are not mere embellishments but are imbedded into the very structure of the song, "Within You and Without You" appears seamless. It stretches, but fits.

What a pity, then, that Harrison's lyrics are dismal and dull. "Love You To," his contribution to *Revolver,* exploded with a passionate sutra quality, but "Within You and Without You" resurrects the very cliches the Beatles helped bury: "With our love/ We could save the world/ If they only knew." All the minor scales in the Orient wouldn't make that profound.

An obsession with production, coupled with a surprising shoddiness in composition, permeates the entire album. John Lennon's raunchiness has become mere caprice in "Being For The Benefit Of Mr. Kite." Paul McCartney's soaring pop magnificats have become politely profound. I find it easier to support those allegations by comparing "She's Leaving Home" with "Eleanor Rigby," because while the musical motifs are similar, a profound sense of tragedy is conveyed in the earlier song through a series of poignantly ironic

vignettes. This expression of agony through triviality has exercised a profound influence on the poetry of rock; you can feel it in Donovan's "Young Girl Blues" and in the BeeGees' stark "New York Mining Disaster."

"She's Leaving Home" is unlikely to influence anyone except the Monkees. Its lyrical technique is uninspired narrative, with a thin icing of irony. All its despair is surface, and so, while "Eleanor Rigby" seethed with implication, "She's Leaving Home" glistens with the flourish of tragedy. Even the instrumentation is explicit in its portrayal of theme. One of the most characteristic things about Beatle music is its intrinsic irony. Orchestration flows from mood; you dig "Norwegian Wood" without even knowing it uses a sitar, because its melancholy moansound fits the mood. "Yesterday" feels baroque on its own melodic terms; it doesn't depend on its arrangement. In both these classic Beatle songs, production follows, never determines, function. But in "She's Leaving Home," harps and strings dominate what are essentially a weak melody and shallow lyrics.

I feel the same about most of the songs on this album. For the first time, the Beatles have given us a package of special effects, dazzling but ultimately fraudulent. In *Revolver,* I found a simplicity and empathy that was staggering. But in *Sergeant Pepper* I sense an obsession with the surrogate magic of production, and a new sarcasm masquerading as cool.

Most distressing, I sense a dangerously dominant sense of what is chic. Much of the radicalism on this album has appeared elsewhere in a less sophisticated form. It was possible months ago to predict the emergence of the extended popsong, because it had already appeared in its infancy (The Fugs: "Virgin Forest"; Love: "Revelation"; The Stones: "Going Home"; Doors: "The End"). The Beach Boys introduced the multimelody with "Good Vibrations" and the Mothers of Invention—not the Beatles—are the pioneers of pop oratorio.

Still the Beatles will probably receive credit for most of the "innovations" on this album, including, of course, the removal of "banding," or space between the cuts. Unfortunately, there is no thematic development to justify this wholeness; at best, the songs are only vaguely related. In unadorned fact, the Beatles had com-

posed a healthy chunk of this material before they thought of centralizing it. Only in mid-production, did the idea of producing an album which would resemble a concert take hold, and the finished product shows this hesitant commitment to the idea of unity. George Harrison's piece has no place in a band concert, and neither do "A Day In The Life" and "Lucy In The Sky."

Still, the cohesive structure of *Sergeant Pepper* cries out for interpretation. I am told that this album is all about the despair of loneliness, but is anxiety really the message we get in "Lovely Rita," "Fixing A Hole," or "A Little Help From My Friends"? Some say the Beatles are head composers. To turn on, goes the reasoning, will admit the enlightened to a whole range of associations and subtleties unfathomable to the straight mind. My experience till now has been that what I like straight, I like all the time. The idea that certain progressions, tonal nuances, and lyrical flights are comprehensible only to the turned-on smacks of critical fascism. I think of the psychedelic experience as an elaboration of a given reality—not a substitute.

The only conceivable way to treat *Sergeant Pepper* would seem to be as caprice. "Sit back and let the evening go." But you and I know the best Beatle music is only deceptively casual. Part of the trouble with this album is its determination to be a game, and the shallowest cop-out is to excuse this work by reporting jubilantly that it has no meaning. It does. In fact some of the songs are soggy with content. The difficulty comes in defining the work as a whole. It is much more sensible to talk of mood than actual meaning in *Sergeant Pepper*. The Beatles have always avoided producing "theme" albums, and despite its quasi-continuity, this one represents no significant break with that tradition. There are no recurrent themes, and only hints of what should have been repeating musical motifs. Nevertheless, this album has a definite mood, even if it is only expressed in its aims. *Rubber Soul* strove for tonal beauty, and it is lushly melodic. *Revolver* attempted to be eclectic; its compositions stand as utterly distinct and self-contained. *Sergeant Pepper* is a circus of sour.

With one important exception, it is precious but devoid of gems. "A Day in the Life" is such a radical departure from the

spirit of the album that it deserves its peninsular position (following the reprise of the "Sergeant Pepper" theme, it comes almost as an afterthought). It has nothing to do with posturing or put-on. It is a deadly earnest excursion in emotive music with a chilling lyric. Its orchestration is dissonant but sparse, and its mood is not whimsical nostalgia but irony.

With it, the Beatles have produced a glimpse of modern city life that is terrifying. It stands as one of the most important Lennon-McCartney compositions, and it is an historic Pop event.

"A Day in the Life" starts with a description of suicide. With the same conciseness displayed in "Eleanor Rigby," the protagonist begins: "I read the news today, oh boy." This mild interjection is the first hint of his disillusionment; compared with what is to follow, it is supremely ironic. "I saw the photograph," he continues, in the voice of a melancholy choir boy:

> He blew his mind out in a car
> He didn't notice that the lights had changed.
> A crowd of people stood and stared
> They'd seen his face before
> Nobody was really sure
> If he was from the House of Lords.

"A Day in the Life" could never make the Top 40, although it may influence a great many songs which do. The aimless, T. S. Eliot-like crowd, forever confronting pain and turning away, will become a common symbol. And its narrator, subdued by the totality of his despair, may reappear in countless compositions as the silent, withdrawn hero.

Musically, there are already indications that "A Day in the Life" is a key to the new music. Electronic-rock, with its aim of staggering an audience, has arrived in half-a-dozen important new releases. None of these songs has the controlled intensity of "A Day in the Life," but the willingness of many restrained musicians to "let go" means that serious aleatory-pop may be on the way.

Ultimately, however, it is the uproar over the alleged influence of drugs on the Beatles which may prevent "A Day in the Life" from reaching the mass audience. The song's refrain, "I'd love to turn you on," has rankled disk jockeys supersensitive to "hidden

subversion" in rock 'n' roll. In fact, a case can be made within the very structure of "A Day in the Life" for the belief that the Beatles —like so many Pop composers—are aware of the highs and lows of consciousness.

The song is built on a series of tense, melancholic passages, followed by soaring releases. In the opening stanza, for instance, John's voice comes near to cracking with despair. But after the invitation, "I'd like to turn you on," the Beatles have inserted an extraordinary atonal thrust which is shocking, even painful, to the ears. But it brilliantly encases the song and, if the refrain preceding it suggests turning on, the crescendo parallels a drug-induced "rush."

The bridge begins in a staccato crossfire. We feel the narrator rising, dressing, and commuting by rote. The music is nervous with the dissonance of cabaret jazz. A percussive drum melts into a panting railroad chug. The words fade into a chant of free, spacious chords, like the initial marijuana "buzz." But the tone becomes mysterious and then ominous. Deep strings take us on a Wagnerian descent and we are back to the original blues theme, and the original declaration, "I read the news today, oh boy."

Actually, it is difficult to see why the BBC banned "A Day in the Life," because its message is, quite clearly, the flight from banality. It describes a profound reality, but it certainly does not glorify it. And its conclusion, though magnificent, seems to represent a negation of self. The song ends on one low, resonant note that is sustained for 40 seconds. Having achieved the absolute peace of nullification, the narrator is beyond melancholy. But there is something brooding and irrevocable about his calm. It sounds like destruction.

What a shame that "A Day in the Life" is only the coda to an otherwise undistinguished collection of work. In substituting the studio conservatory for an audience, the Beatles have lost crucial rapport, and that emptiness at the roots is what makes their new album a monologue. Nothing is real therein, and nothing to get hung about. Too bad; I have a sweet tooth for reality. I like my art drenched in it, and even from fantasy, I expect authenticity. What I worship about the Beatles is their forging of rock into what is real. It made them artists; it made us fans; and it made me think like a critic when I turned on my radio.

We still need the Beatles, not as cloistered composers, but as companions. And they still need us, to teach them how to be real again.

—THE NEW YORK TIMES and
THE VILLAGE VOICE, 1967

# ● MAGICAL MYSTERY RAP

We were all there, combed and coiffed and standing in a row munching cocktail gossip, having just passed a security clearance in triplicate. It felt good getting checked off on so many lists and knowing you were not "unofficial." So we stood around rapping, terribly nervous all the while because this was a magic press conference, with two real Beatles scheduled to appear.

Every month there is at least one magic press conference in New York. That's the one at which you don't notice the bar. Sometimes it is held for the society slicks or the political press (though candidates seldom provide "magic" in public moments because their privacy is so accessible to the press). Sometimes it is called to celebrate that public rattling of bones known as Militants Scourge the Honkies. Occasionally you go to hear someone announce a nervous breakdown, a lawsuit, or a divorce.

Usually these are vapid events, with most of the electricity provided by the mere presence of the great, not by what they say. But there is a certain dynamism in the very act of royalty addressing representatives of the common herd. Reporters are sensitive to variations in this ritual; any superstar who dares to break role by being sincerely friendly at a magic press conference might as well hand in his image at the door.

Usually you can tell a Magical Mystery Rap is at hand by the total lack of any advance information. The appropriate people are

informed just before the event, by telegram, messenger, or pre-
arranged word of mouth. In the case of the Beatles' visit to New
York phones rang incessantly along the pop-line and all you got
on the other end was relief at not being left out alone. Finally the
telegrams arrived, and then the press passes, and then the great
event.

"They're right behind that door," said one cellophane copybopper
clutching a steno pad to her non-breast.

"How can you tell?" asked her best friend, eyeliner aflutter.

"I can smell the pot."

And so we took seats around a long dais, and listened to Derek
Taylor announce that the Beatles were here to talk about Apple.
Now, Derek Taylor is only the ace publicist of the Western World.
His presence alone might make us applaud the news that Tokyo
Rose was contemplating a comeback along the Veterans hospital
circuit. Today he looked lean and haggard but not inefficient. First
still photographers, he was saying, and then reporters, and then
radio and television. "What we're having today is a press conference and not a war," he surmised. "We used to do this in the
old days—when we toured the world. When we were young."

Then the doors opened and out they marched, encased in a
cloud of aftertaste. Three years ago we would all have gone leaping
up the aisles in Shea Stadium ecstasy, but today we were trying
to treat them as cultural equals. Mere heroes. Was that a wrinkle
over Paul's brow, or just a smudge where he held his finger? Were
those bags under his eyes, as he made a pretty pout for the cameras,
or just shadow? Was that dye in John Lennon's sandy hair? And
those round glasses hanging over his nose, could they perhaps be
bi-focals?

But no, the Beatles were for real. Paul smirked as the cameras
snapped all around him, lkie the clicking of innumerable tongues.
John slouched in his chair like a juvenile delinquent who has just
found himself appointed chief of police. A lady with Conde-Nast
writen in rouge across her cheeks said, "They walked right by me,
and I didn't even scream." A man in a Nehru jacket told a balding
reporter, "The one on the left is John, and Paul is on the right."
And a girl in boots that seemed to come up to her armpits observed,
"Isn't it funny how we never get used to them?"

Then the questions began, with a silent flapping of hands. John thought the Maharishi was a mistake but found truth in his teachings. Paul observed that it was fine for a Beatle to err, because "We're human." Then he added, "We thought the Maharishi wasn't." Both admitted that they still meditate "now and then" because, said John, "it seems to be nice, like brushing your teeth." At least he didn't giggle.

Then the questions began in earnest, traversing the familiar what's-wrong-with-our-youth terrain and finally settling down to relevant personal data (i.e., "How often do you turn on, John?" "It's happening all the time").

There was no McCarthy supporter to ask whether Lennon would go clean for Gene, and Jerry Rubin was not present to ask about the relevance of Mao to "Eleanor Rigby." Nary a reference was made to that staple of past Beatle press conference, sex and the single walrus, and nobody asked why the Beatles wore long hair. So the boys got off lightly. But nobody seemed very interested in Apple either. The Beatles' new mystery corporation, which will centralize their interests in film, records, fashion, electronics, and even publishing, was hardly mentioned at the conference. Of course, it all sounded impressive, but it was strange to realize that the Beatles were in town on a business trip. With a private interview for *Business Week*. And Paul sitting there in a black pin-stripe suit looking mercantile and a little bored. For his part, John was vague about what Apple was or what it would do. "We want to set up a situation so people can make a film without getting down on their knees in somebody's office—probably yours."

Before it was over, I asked about their reaction to English press criticism of their recent television show. "They expected a tinselly Christmas thing," John said. "Whatever image of us they have, if we don't fulfill it, they're disappointed." Someone asked about their next record. "It'll be all right, the next one, don't worry," said Paul, rather shyly. "A record like any other would smell as sweet," John explained.

When they left, we smiled at each other and agreed that it had been magical after all. I didn't try for a private audience, because I thought they'd be too hassled to say anything meaningful and because I suspected that they wouldn't like me. I prefer to keep,

as a souvenir of their trip, the point during their television appearance when the man who was substituting for Johnny Carson
asked John Lennon why he was nervous, and John looked around
at the formica props in that pseudo-living room and answered
"Because it's unnatural."

—THE VILLAGE VOICE, 1968

# ● NOTHING IS REVEALED

*John Wesley Harding* goes Susan Sontag one better. It not only eludes, but dares interpretation. It sits like a heavy lead safe guarding its precious innards with bolts of cryptic cool. Reach for the handle and it seems to hiss from within itself: "I am inscrutable." Give the lock an undaunted shove, and it taunts, "I may be empty after all."

Bob Dylan writes shields around himself. His imagery, his voice, even his album jacket keep us intrigued but distant. Stop to think about his songs and they grab you by the neck—strangling, slashing, putting you on. The put on has become such a virile form of self-defense that we prefer it to pursuing meaning. We love to watch a great poser like Dylan making magic charades. It's so easy to experience a joke when the victim is a square Other.

But Dylan is so much more than the sum of his plumage. His hip mazes always lead somewhere. Beyond the image-barriers, they trace a direct path to the quiet, afraid softness at the center of all his hoodlum-saints. Dylan's major theme is human vulnerability. His images repeat the same inner message over and over like a rock mantra: "I need, I have needed, I will need."

There is need in the least likely corners of a Dylan song: nasty need in "Like a Rolling Stone," angry need in "Hard Rain's Gonna Fall," real need in "Sad-Eyed Lady of the Lowlands." To dwell on Dylan's provocations is to miss his want.

In 1963 he instructed Nat Hentoff, who wrote the liner notes for *The Freewheelin' Bob Dylan:* "Whatever else you say about me, everything I do and sing and write comes out of me." If it is true that he is a spokesman for my generation, it is because he is first and always a poet of himself. This is what he has been telling us from the start. He said it best in the jacket-poem on *Bringing It All Back Home:* "a song is anything that can walk by itself / i am a songwriter. a poem is a naked person . . . some people say that I am a poet." *

Three years after that occasional verse, he is saying it again. Standing in a Woodstock forest in the same suede jacket he wore for the cover of *Blonde on Blonde,* he is back with a new deck of myths, a new series of threats, and a new set of revelations.

Chief among the myths is an alleged re-emergence of Bob Dylan the folksinger. True, *John Wesley Harding* is a first-glance throwback to those dear, dead, acoustic days. The blues organ which once gave shape to his savagery has been muted, and the guitars have been unplugged, their shimmering tones reduced to a sedate whisper.

But this album is no *Freewheelin' Dylan Revisited.* Its music is not the purposely primitive sound of early Dylan. The indiscriminate harmonica fills on his first albums have become sharp, distinct statements. And his voice, once as indefinite as an unpunctuated sentence, is now a sturdy, sustaining instrument.

The pudgy kid in boots and blue jeans who howled "Blowin' in the Wind" is not the man who croons "I'll Be Your Baby Tonight." In fact, the arrangements of *John Wesley Harding* make no attempt to recapture or redefine folk music. The modest rhythm section (drums, bass, an occasional piano), the sedate backbeat, and the deliberately lowered volume are all there to distinguish Dylan's sound from the cataclysmic sputtering we associate with pop music. If the music on *John Wesley Harding* sounds primitive, it is only because we have come to regard anything that blows the middle ear as rock. In thumbing his harp at the psychedelic comintern, Dylan also introduces us to a more audible sound, best expressed in the supple chording and sparse lyric of "Down Along the Cove."

* © Witmark Music.

Much has been made of his journey to Nashville to record *John Wesley Harding*. But "Blonde on Blonde" was cut there too. Flying Al Kooper south doesn't make country music. But attention to detail in composition and a careful selection of sidemen (always a point of pride with Dylan) do. As Robert Shelton wrote in his *New York Times* review, the ghost writer on this album is Hank Williams. But Dylan's attitude toward C & W music is respectful, not imitative. If *John Wesley Harding* borrows freely from the conventions of country, it is no faithful recreation of the Nashville sound. Its intent seems to be nostalgia. Dylan's voice is braced against a throbbing steel guitar. His imagery is simple and domestic. His voice is a mossy bank of reminiscence.

What he has to say, however, is anything but sentimental. Dylan confronts a cliché the way a butcher eyes a chicken. His new songs abound with slaughtered platitudes. They provide the humor in "The Ballad of Frankie Lee and Judas Priest," and they fill "I'll Be Your Baby Tonight" with the kind of gentle parody that brings it all back to life.

Dylan's much-heralded alliance with country music—like his embrace of rock three years ago—is more a matter of exploration than entrenchment. He has learned to use form as a means; he adapts the conventions of one style to investigate the possibilities of another. That, in essence, was the transfusion he gave Woody Guthrie's songs at a Carnegie Hall benefit recently. He goosed "Grand Coolie Dam" and "Mrs. Roosevelt" awake, infusing their time tattered verses with howling, hip-grinding, rockabilly raunch.

Dylan's achievements as a lyric poet are perpetually debated, but little attention has been paid to his abilities as a composer or as an interpreter of other people's material. At Carnegie Hall he modestly imposed himself upon the music of Woody Guthrie. In *John Wesley Harding* he imposes himself upon his own roots.

Much of the confusion about "old" and "new" Dylans on this album stems from his use of traditional phrases and melodies. "As I Went Out One Morning" sounds like one of those migrating Scottish-Appalachian ballads, with its entwining narrative and archaic language. ("I spied the fairest damsel"..."Depart from me this moment") But Dylan begins to mold the conventional structure to suit his own purposes from the moment he touches it. Strange

modernisms creep into the dialogue. ("I beg you sir, she pleaded /
From the corners of her mouth / I will secretly accept you / And
together we'll fly South")* By the time this song ends, our mountain ballad has become a weird non-love song, as timeless as anything Dylan has ever written. He conveys this mood through form
as well as content, and that additional dimension adds immense
depth and irony to all the songs on *John Wesley Harding*. They
are not folk tunes, although their roots are apparent.

As a folksinger, Dylan never questioned stylistic devices. His
songs usually landed like open parachutes, melody and lyric structure falling where they might. But now he is concerned with putting
a song in its proper setting, and this kind of modal self-awareness
is antithetical to the spirit of folk music.

Well, true, *John Wesley Harding* is a series of juxtapositions—
sometimes playful, sometimes dramatic—of form against function.
But it is also an album filled with good songs.

Those who would proclaim that Dylan has deserted poetry
should consider exactly what was left out and what went into *John
Wesley Harding*. Certainly the scansion is no less irregular, the
language no less awkward than it was on *Blonde on Blonde*. What
is missing here is the amassing of detail which once characterized a
Dylan composition. Now, his authorship is a subtler thing. His
songs, once epics of qualification, have become declarative statements. Their lines are short, sharpened blades.

In any other writer, this attention to structure, coupled with a
broader concept of how a song should convey its meaning, would
be received as a sign of artistic growth. But Dylan is most widely
remembered for his excesses in style and substance. This album
will shock those who know Dylan only as the possessor of a
wondrous set of verbal antlers. It was meant to do just that: to
show his independence from the rock-baroque style he invented.

But the barren poetry of *John Wesley Harding* is thoroughly
appropriate. Many of these songs are really tales, sung against a
backbeat. If Dylan's language sounds merely descriptive, it is
because he lets the action speak for itself. His sly, sparse imagery
forces us to react to incidents and situations, not just to observations. Once we have abandoned the idea of "poetry," it works

* C-Dwarf Music Co.

incognito, bringing a mood of profound apprehension to this album.

That tone has always been present in Dylan's work. His people have hardly changed. Even when triumphant, they are tormented; at peace, they await fear. His themes too have remained constant. Songs like "The Wicked Messenger" and "Last Night I Saw Saint Augustine" seem to spring from "Desolation Row"—Dylan's rock apocalypse. The line from "Subterranean Homesick Blues" to "The Ballad of Frankie Lee and Judas Priest" almost draws itself. The moral of both songs is "Don't follow leaders / Watch the parking meters."

Even the outlaw saints who dominate this album have been a part of Dylan's song scene from the start. The most poignant image in "Sad-Eyed Lady of the Lowlands" captures its heroine "with the child of a hoodlum wrapped up in your arms." Even earlier, in "Outlaw Blues," Dylan observed, "I may look like Robert Ford, but I feel just like Jesse James." But the brooding observer who narrated Dylan's songs in the past has become a participant in *John Wesley Harding*.

"There must be some way out of here," he begins in "All Along the Watchtower." That is no mere observation, but the start of a direct confrontation between two men deeply involved in its outcome. They leap from one non sequitur to another, but there is an inescapable sense of struggle between their lines. Why, and for what stakes, Dylan never says. But the very atmosphere around them is charged with the imminent arrival of something inevitable, absolute, and evil.

How tempting to add three dots to the last word in this song; it is so utterly unfinished. All the details rush us toward an apocalypse that never happens (except, perhaps, off camera). Instead, the final stanza leaves us stranded in the scenery, waiting for what? why? where? Is this climax death, or does it only seem deadly? An agonized harmonica shrieks under its breath "nothing is revealed!"

But everything is implied. "All Along the Watchtower" is Dylan's first vision of personal extinction. His characters have never before encountered death, but on this album they begin to consider the possibility. Their tales are brief, visceral debates with existence.

A poet reveals his time through himself; Bob Dylan is his own

motif. So listen for the outlaw-confessor in *John Wesley Harding*. Under the suede smile, he is still naked. Take up his dare to be interpreted. The man who misses most is not the one who makes foolish guesses, but he who refrains from guessing at all.

—THE VILLAGE VOICE, 1968

# ● ARETHA AROUSES

I admit I am only a reluctant connoisseur of rhythm and blues. I find white phrasing easier to take, and I feel on safer ground in separating the valid from the vulgar when the artist is making use of conventions I understand.

But the soul revival has made it possible for me to approach black pop with a good deal less cultural feedback. Though my most apparent reaction to the r & b presence has been a tendency to listen harder to white blues groups like the Butterfield Band, I feel less and less like the drama critic who praises a Broadway musical as being "good for what it is," and more like a true listener, participating in the sound.

Classic blues is harder for me to get into. It takes a great deal more patience to extend my own reference points into, say, Bukkha White. It's the same feeling I get forcing myself to swallow jazz—I do it for educational reasons, because it is there and important. But it lacks immediacy for me. I know Billie Holliday is great, but she only seems sentimental. I know Coltrane is a master, but he sounds like a butcher. So I listen, unmoved and ungrooved, and I tell myself it must take suave to be a jazz critic.

I've spent a lot of ear-time lately hearing a four-record collection of Bessie Smith's songs from Columbia. But I have trouble separating the singer from the sound. She is Bessie Smith all right. Albee heroine and grandmother of us all, and she gives messages

to Janis Joplin from the great beyond. But listening to her only feels like ancestor worship. There are moments of gritty power in her voice, but I am lulled by passage after passage of old music. Closing my eyes (because, as I learned in California, that is the way to *hear*), I can only think of a Farmer Gray cartoon, with barnyard animals frolicking to a Bessie Smith soundtrack.

But then there is Aretha Franklin. She drops notes on me like a raincloud. Not always, but sometimes, I sit there listening to her bend sounds—tickling, coaxing them—as though she were sculpting, not singing. Even when I've heard "Respect" 50 times, it picks me up at 5 A.M.

She is a sexy lady. "Doctor Feelgood" has precious little to do with the AMA. Her "Natural Woman" doesn't get that way from a laxative. And her "Satisfaction" is the first black version of that song that adds anything to Mick Jagger's delivery for me. Mick may have been "trying to make some girl who tells me, baby, better come back—maybe next week," but Aretha changes just a few clauses in that statement and makes "Satisfaction" a study in sexuality, not hard luck.

*Aretha Arrives* reminds me of the sound I used to search for on Sunday night—late, when no rock was on the radio. After I'd found it on some station broadcasting from the bayous of Jersey, I'd lie back and try to figure how something so reverent could also be filthy and wonderful.

—THE VILLAGE VOICE, 1967

# ● ELECTRIC MINOTAUR

Pop culture moves in perfect waves (this just happens to be the undertow). Whenever the current fails to provide a natural momentum, the record industry offers itself as the agent of propulsion. Prophets flash the message of the moment, but they don't create it. That happens at penthouse level, where style and supply both follow demand, and the search for next year's superstar resembles a great white grope.

This little system (sign 'em in June; sell 'em by November) has haunted pop music far longer than I have. It proceeds with the accustomed ease of ritual. The summer's catch of greasy groovers must be cleaned and packaged—all according to mode. October is trend month, when those little red bullets in Cashbox begin to hit home. Of course, there is a solid core of record executives who realize that personal vision is what makes rock vital. But no one who tries his hand at sounding out the zeitgeist and making it sell, is immune to the charms of lady trend.

No wonder even the most enlightened of company freaks is turning a lighter shade of pale. The direction this season seems to be none at all. We're supposed to be in the middle of a great blues revival. Albert King totes the white man's electric burden, and it's Aretha Franklin at the barricades (in sequins—right?). Well, I don't know. Maybe, we can't overcome, but we can win medals

together. We can loot together. And last spring's orgy of assassinations proved we could act as guests at each other's wakes.

But about music which seethes the savage beast, I don't know. No doubt this fall will see the elevation of at least one honky-blues supergroup (for quality's sake, I hope it's Canned Heat). Already the crowds at the Fillmore East are creaming over any cat in a workshirt who sweats black and knows how to put 12 bars together. Muddy Waters has surfaced as soul guru of the movement, with an album called "Electric Mud," (Chess) which manages in at least three places to sound like Muddy Waters imitating the Rolling Stones imitating Muddy Waters. Money may change hands over such alliances, and music may change heads. But I don't think we're ready to dig the same sound on 125th Street and Saint Mark's Place. Prove me wrong. Go out and buy Archie Bell and the Drells and sock it to me.

Last summer's rock revival failed to produce a single group worthy of serious consideration (with the exception of Ten Years After, which used the oldie concept as a springboard for its own fantastic be-bop blend). Country music (which was supposed to lead the way back and around) comes on in a Nehru jacket fringed with buckskin. There is the Band. There is Moby Grape. And there is the Byrds' album, "Sweetheart Of The Rodeo," a gentle, moving work, and the most authentic piece of nostalgia in a year when every folkie worth his Little Sandy Review is going Nashville. I play that album continuously; it's melted into my mind like a Country "Rubber Soul." I'm under no illusions about its "soul." There is a very evident attempt to stylize a musical tradition afoot here, but it comes off with such sincerity that the entire album (cover and all) is carried beyond the realm of camp. The music is supple and mellow, the sigh-singing warmly harmonic, and the random riffs (by some of Nashville's finest) first rate.

It's crucial to consider the origin of every cut on this remarkable album. There are Guthrie standards, country chartbusters, creaking hymns, and Dylan originals. That all these diverse elements (and even a delicate California ballad by Graham Parsons, called "Hickory Wind") could be integrated without condescension is a major accomplishment. That and the ease with which it all rolls across your mind.

I suspect that the resiliency of the Byrds has as much to do with the shape the scene is in as with their own skill. Such longevity in jazz is not unusual, but from a pop group it is truly uncanny. Yet it seems to fit an emerging pattern in rock. This year's major excitement has been provided by established titans (Dylan, the Beatles, the Stones, the Airplane, et al). Beneath them, the creative ferment which once propelled rock beyond its own expectations has disappeared. Not since the Dick Clark '50s has there been less turbulence in pop. We know who we like and we want to keep them on top. We'd better, because who's going to take their place?

Certainly, no beginning group has produced an album with anything like the sheer force of "Crown Of Creation." Forget complexity, experience, and Maurice on the 12-track. Song by song, this latest Jefferson Airplane album is a solid piece of excitement, and easily the best work the group has ever done. "After Bathing At Baxters" was muddled by over-attention to detail at the expense of things like melody and lyric cohesion. It was stuffy, undefined, and spoiled. But here is a superbly lyrical album, confident and involving. After this album, you have to consider Grace Slick one of the finest stylists in rock. Her lyrics for "Lather" are wistful and melancholic. And her singing on "Triad" is strident without being Streisand.

What we have received from the Airplane and the Byrds is both a personal reaffirmation and a crucial sign that nothing is happening underneath. Rock is affected by an evident discontinuity, and this is where the industry emerges as creator of the very trends it seeks so solemnly to follow.

Even our best albums are familiar landscapes. The terrain has been thoroughly explored, the roads are excellent, the natives friendly. The journey is stimulating, but uneventful.

In that sense, Jimi Hendrix's new album, "Electric Ladyland" (Warner Brothers) is a musical freeway. You come away feeling that it's overlong, indiscriminate, and needlessly jammed. But beyond these first impressions—which are an inescapable part of the Jimi Hendrix experience—it is clearly a major artery. Hendrix's phrasing is as powerful, his musical presence as persistent as ever. And he remains one awful lyricist.

But what matters most about this album is its production. In the

studio, Hendrix turns out to be his own best editor. (He's listed as "producer and director," which means, I assume, that he holds all movie rights.) For sheer texture, this is an uncanny piece of sound-collage. It comes at you whining, sighing, or curling its lip in arrogant dismay. There are Cream stains, Beatle tracks, and fumes of Airplane exhaust, but somehow it comes off as pastiche rather than plagiarism. There are also a lot of celebrity sidemen present and accounted for here (Buddy Miles, Al Kooper, Stevie Winwood, and Jack Cassidy). The supercombo idea in rock strikes me as one enormous shuck, not just because I despise the drooling eagerness with which some pop musicians approach the treasure-house of jazz, but because very little good music has come out of this arrangement. On "Super Session," for example, I like what Kooper and Stills do with "It Takes A Lot To Laugh," but the rest is far less interesting than anything these cats have laid down in their respective groups.

But the Hendrix album is another scene. I suspect the reason why his all-star lineup works is the firmly established subservience his back-up musicians must inevitably accept. No one short of Joseph Stalin could upstage Jimi Hendrex, and backed by even the most distinctive rock stylists, it is his guitar we hear first—loud and together.

Dig how this works in "Voodoo Child," the album's strongest cut and probably the finest rock appreciation of blues you'll ever hear. Hendrix is always out there, like an electric minotaur, flaying away at the business of being absurdly black with the kind of groovy contempt the English call Flash. And, Jumpin' Jack, that word was made for the Jimi Hendrix Experience.

When I think about my most gratuitous errors as a critic, I can never escape my early outrage at Hendrix's vulgarity. Well, he does pander to his audience, and it does feel humiliating. Coming from a white man (Morrison cum Jagger), I could have easily accepted that jingle-jangle grace. But I still demand dignity from a black performer (the difference between Otis Redding and Wilson Pickett, or between Odetta and James Brown). It's possible to excuse that criterion as a holdover from folk-music, where blacks were allowed to be rebellious as long as they were saintly as well. But it runs far deeper into the kind of adjustment I had to make as a white man

to the presence of aggressive (i.e., impolite) blacks. It is still very hard for me to accept a black man who enjoys his own vulgarity. I can take the Panthers, with their cool aggression, or the preachers, with their Christian charity. But Hendrix is a jiver, in the most threatening sense. Disguised as the corrupt black Prince—Othello's Revenge—he is a mirror-image of our own inner darkies, struggling to be clownish, sexual, and free. Maybe that's why Jimi Hendrix is so much less relevant to black culture. Ultimately, his is a message blacks got long ago: everybody is his own spade.

—THE VILLAGE VOICE, 1968

# ● TALK OF ROCK
# RIALTO

Van Dyke Parks might have grown old in comfortable obscurity. At 25, he had made his mark along Sunset Boulevard (California's teflon-pan alley) as the producer of moderately successful pop groups such as Harper's Bizarre and the Mojo Men. His clients never quite achieved superstardom, but their very presence on the top 40 charts gave Van Dyke access to the burgeoning Los Angeles rock scene. He appeared incognito on a few hip albums. He provided lyrics for some of the Beach Boys' most fascinating songs. His sly, elliptical verse gained him an ecstatic following of his own.

But few in Van Dyke's coterie imagined that he could ever become the talk of the rock rialto, with a debut album called *Song Cycle* rivaling transcendental meditation as the pop phenomenon one *must* have an opinion of. In the first place, producers are traditionally "invisible men" on the pop scene, doomed to lead lives of anonymous wealth. And besides, Van Dyke looks more like an usher than a superstar. There is no hairy demon behind his smile, no evil in his childface.

On a visit to New York, he greets you in his room at the Plaza with patrician reserve. He takes your coat, opens the curtain upon a hero's view of Central Park, and offers you a skinny cigarette. Right away, you notice his glasses (horn-rimmed) and his nose (far too demure for a superstar). He starts to speak and you observe his shoulders, which fill a flowered shirt like wire hangers. Long

171

underwear shows below his cuffs. Superstars don't wear long johns, you mutter in dismay.

But the same audience that has transported rock from the dance floor to the concert hall is elevating a new breed of celebrities who can think. If Van Dyke lacks physical charisma, he is cerebral enough to inspire a growing cult of writers, musicians, and beautiful people with serious faces. His album, *Song Cycle,* turns them on because it is studded with musical allusions like a charm bracelet.

Van Dyke quotes profusely from a galaxy of greats: Ives, Mahler, Debussy, and Beethoven. But he approaches these men as a listener, not a scholar. He blends their styles (and actual music) into a freewheeling collage of sounds, phrases, and motifs. But these "classical" touches are merely the underpinnings of *Song Cycle.* The album's dominant theme is Southern California—in all its saucy pseudo-reality.

"I wanted to capture my environment," Van Dyke explains. "I tried to invent phrases which would sound familiar even though they really weren't." With a relish of American pop forms, he juxtaposes Chuck Berry and Paul Whiteman. A verse of "Nearer My God To Thee" brushes against a passage which seems to have been extracted from a Busby Berkeley musical. One song, "By the People," features a chorus like the Andrews Sisters, a violin solo dripping with glissandos, traces of courtly-dance music, a coda in the impressionist vein, and a finale of cannons and churchbells.

Over orchestration like this, Van Dyke relates (in that sly warble which is his singing voice) the strangest libretto ever to grace the vocal track of a pop album. His lyrics bristle with puns and para-clichés. An uninitiated listener must do battle with each song's syntax to extract its precise meaning. But it is far simpler to approach this cycle as a series of autobiographical sketches. It's the story of Van Dyke's migration West, of what he found and how he made it.

For many, *Song Cycle* is an enormous put-on, the latest in an endless string of camp-follies. It may yet run in an off-off-Broadway coffee house, but Van Dyke Parks couldn't be more serious about his dream-landscape. He first saw Hollywood in 1955 as a child actor (he still remembers being driven to the studio in a limousine), and he has been fascinated by its magic ever since. Though his own

photo appears on the album's jacket, he originally envisioned "a study of the Hollywood hills—you know, the kind of country where Gloria Swanson went riding in her car." He beams at the mention of her name.

He was born in 1943, far from Sunset Boulevard, on a military base in Mississippi. When the family moved to Pennsylvania, he studied piano and composition at the Carnegie Institute of Technology. He says he was "a poor student and a frequent truant." He insists that his experiences playing clarinet at Polish weddings influenced him more than his education. But when Van Dyke returned to Hollywood as a record producer in 1961, he possessed a far sturdier musical foundation than most of his competitors. He was able to absorb the rules of commercial success without being engulfed by them. ("What drags me most about pure rock," he explains, "is that it has all these things going about being nitty-gritty, and yet it's encrusted with chic.") He began to compose when the pop market was devouring creative innovation with an eclectic frenzy. On *Song Cycle* he found an ideal showcase for his musical idiosyncrasies and for his perplexing parenthetical lyrics:

> A Southwester in the yard invested with the garden
> And camped in concentration of a tall lilac
> To peel the rust off purple arbor.
> Time is not the main thought from under the rain wrought
> From roots that brought us coots to hoot and haul
> Us all back to the prime ordeal.
> Dust off Pearl Harbor time.*

Like his verse, Van Dyke's conversation flows in a gentle parabola over a landscape of ideas. He doesn't touch, but alights upon a subject. The only question he tackles with any consistency is the matter of style. He considers taste tantamount to grace, and identical with art. "I'm interested in understatement," he says. "I don't think it's proper to dominate your audience. I'm trying to stand gracefully, and even to control my presence, without dominating. Through the use of creative energy, I want to give people an excuse to trust me, and pay me."

A strange goal for a superstar-to-be. But *Song Cycle* is a brilliant

* Reprinted with permission of the writer.

realization of just those standards. It mirrors a wider spectrum of American musical culture than anyone had thought possible within a pianissimo setting—and it does it tastefully. In fact, not since Gershwin has someone so completely involved in the pop holocaust emerged with such a transcendent concept of what American music really means. *Song Cycle* is that album we have all been waiting for: an auspicious debut, a stunning work of pop art, a vital piece of Americana, and a damned good record to boot.

—THE NEW YORK TIMES, 1968

# • ART ROCK:
# YEAR OF THE
# MINI-MAGNIFICAT

Those of you who have been flitting from country hoedown to gospel jamboree in search of the "new thing" can rest easy. You can stop brushing off those old Jerry Lee Lewis records because you've heard they're worth something in England now. No need to break your toes getting into position to play the Danelectro sitar, either. Let those minor scales fall from your eyes. Bone up on the ol' Toccata and Frug instead. This month's successor to psychedelic razzmatazz is art-rock.

Not that we weren't warned 10 years ago, when Chuck Berry wailed: "Roll over Beethoven and give Tchaikovsky the news." But who could have thought the rock revolution would lead its children to the very gates of High Culture, where they could proceed to peel off the gold paint and sell it as Art? I'm thinking of that mound of thought-Jell-O called *Days of Future Passed* which features the Moody Blues, The London Festival Orchestra, and lots of bad poetry.

A little background: The Moodys are a fine rock band, whose wailing sound dates back to the dawn of Beatlemania. But these days, rock groups change images like a woman discarding nylons. In their new incarnation, the Moodys give us ponderous songs with titles like "Dawn Is a Feeling" and "Forever Afternoon (Tuesday?)." True, there are some stunning string parts on this record, some superb vocalizing, and one haunting ballad called "Nights in

White Satin." But even this song is rendered obtuse by the kind of hyper-orchestration that leaves you in the balcony waiting for the movie to begin (I find myself muttering things over the music, like "Look, Natasha, Moscow burns . . ."). This DeMillian effect is re-enforced every time that sepulchral voice intones a heroic couplet or two ("Lonely man cries for love and has none. . . . Senior citizens wish they were young"). The CIA may someday find a use for lines like these, in wringing confessions from Allen Ginsberg, for instance. But those of us who cherish our freedom from faddery will join in paraphrasing the old dictum, "Art is long, and patience short."

Not that the Moody Blues are the only pop group to become fossilized in the current embrace of classicism. Consider the National Gallery which makes a dismal attempt to capture the paintings of Paul Klee (the ads tell you how to pronounce his name) in a rock setting. Observe the Rotary Connection, conjuring up ornate arrangements of rock standards that remind me of the Radio City Music Hall at Easter. Meet the Nice, a new English group whose organist manages to make Khatchaturian's Sabre Dance sound like "I Must Go Where the Wild Goose Goes." Or take the Vanilla Fudge. Their latest Marshmallow-drama features an organ-drenched eulogy for Beethoven, which carries the mind not to Germany in the 19th century, but to Hoboken in 1958.

Yes, the beat does go on, albeit laden with pomp, circumstance, and an occasional mini-magnificat. And those unfortunate men whose job it is to promote classical music among the masses have not failed to notice a new potential market for their goods. If Ravi Shankar could find a place in young America's thumping heart, they reason, why not Bela Bartok, or Erik Satie? Just last week, I received a button reading "I'm on to Erik Satie" which I intend to wear at all political rallies. And not long ago, I noticed an ad in a trade magazine, placed by no less gray an eminence than the Deutsche Grammophon company. Hippies "dig" Mozart, it announced. As if to drive the point home to skeptics, it displayed a bust of the master adorned with shades, beads and flowers. All it lacked was some pertinent graffiti scrawled across the forehead.

I do think there is honest ground for cross-fertilization in pop music. After all, a classic is something that remains relevant be-

yond its time. What I object to is not the utilization of time-honored themes and forms in rock, but their reduction to the level of addenda. There is a profound difference between the picture-postcard classicism of the National Gallery, and the real-life vitality of Procol Harum. Most of the current art-rockers owe an unacknowledged debt to this English group, which first jolted the pop scene with potent blues interpretations of classical motifs. Their best-known single, "A Whiter Shade of Pale," is actually a set of rocking variations on a Bach cantata. On their only album, the group's organist, Charles Matthew Fischer, displays his virtuosity in a fierce tour of a music student's psyche called "Repent Walpurgis." This piece, which conjures up images of the Romantic masters without even making us feel we are hearing imitation-Art, is the most staggering art-rock instrumental to date. Fischer's organ soars and coaxes, while a stinging blues guitar slashes up the melody into glowing embers of sound.

I suspect that Procol Harum's unique vitality in transposing the classics comes from genuine involvement. As a serious student, Fischer must "feel" Bach the way Aretha Franklin "feels" gospel. Now, a group called Ars Nova has released its debut album on Elektra, and listening, I can feel the same kind of involvement. These, too, are music students, and their album is filled with extra-curricular energy. A trumpet skips merrily over 500 years of music, stopping here in the High Renaissance, there in Dixieland, and finally at the head of a grand processional. Wherever Ars Nova wanders, you can sense a thorough rapport with the forms they employ. When they touch a piece of music, it responds. "Pavan for My Lady" brings spring in Central Park to the Renaissance chanson. "Album in Your Mind" makes Kurt Weill's songs into battle cries again. And Ars Nova's "Zarathustra" is far more than Richard Strauss in hippy drag. The group retains the original's glorious sense of melodrama, but adds a joyous modernity that falls just this side of parody. Thundering drums puncture those paunchy rhythms. Blazing brass breathes fire into that asbestos melody. Oh, to march down the aisle at Graduation to *this* "Zarathustra!"

Ars Nova is the first rock group since Procol Harum to convey, through classical themes, its own reality. If there is any problem with this album, it is that the group seems too involved in staking

out its roots to play anything approaching straight rock. Its more conventional songs sound worse than ordinary. But small complaint: Ars Nova shows us the way to a pop music that is artistic without being arty. They may not be psychedelic (I'll have to ask my guru, who is also a promo man, about that) but they sure do blow my mind.

—NEW YORK MAGAZINE, 1968

# ● WHY THE BLUES?

Black cloud crossed my mind
Blue mist round my soul
Feel so suicidal
Even hate my rock and roll

—THE BEATLES
*"Yer Blues"*

Steve Paul's Scene has changed a bit, grown stern and funky like the rest of us. I hadn't been there in, say, six weeks. I can't explain why. It's as a good a place to hear music as any in this promopolis. But I've been hanging loose lately; I suppose that means staying home, soaking in the feel of all my interiors. My head is unsettled, but not confused. Singing the praises of pop seems to resemble a kind of futile nationalism to me now. All my bags are packed, and I'm casing out frontiers, trying to choose the best point to make a border crossing.

Is that feeling endemic to the underground, or are we all looking to break our leases? If you're a journalist that might mean dropping your column. If you're a musician, you might cut your hair, rip away those psychedelic chevrons, and dig roots.

You can't listen to today's rock without noticing the sound of shovels. We are churning up the earth again, with the aim of re-fertilization, but with the immediate effect of killing off what

happens to be growing—however poorly—at the time. Pop, of course, is all topsoil. It's what shows—immediately, apparently. It catches the sun and receives the rain, and erodes first under the impact of trampling feet. I once chose to live off this topsoil because for a time, it was lovely to look at, and rich to the touch. As for the bedrock, I was satisfied to perceive that it offered vital support. But the surface was what turned me on.

Well, the old mind-garden is a little arid these days. The topsoil has been thinned by non-stop harvesting, and hardened by an early political frost. Your average love-child is beginning to resemble the better half of "American Gothic." Time to dream the dustbowl again. We are all Okies, so bring on the great depression. Time to wrap our perceptions into a cocoon. Time to retire to the country. Time to worship the revolution (It's got a good beat, and y'can dance to it). Anything to avoid another chorus of "River Deep, Mountain High" punctuated with rhythm riffs from "Thus Spake Zarathustra." Leave the popspeak to the culturemeisters. They can create a sound, but they cannot make it matter.

The blues matters because it is always there when you need it— those 12 bars inviolate, self-contained, eternal. Blues is the humus of American music, but you have to burrow to find it. When the surface seems to shine of its own accord, all that spadework seems unnecessary. When pop is vital, we are unwilling to sanctify the blues. But rob rock of its spasm-grace, and replace energy with stylized motif, and suddenly, they are turning the topsoil under for nourishment from below.

The blues revival we are witnessing now is a requiem for rock. The simple fact is that the entire pop renaissance of the mid-'60s has failed to sustain itself beyond that first, shattering tonal wave. That failure holds true far beyond the sphere of music. The pop sensibility—and its extensions in painting, theatre, cinema, even politics—never moved from a mere fascination with the surface of things, toward a true metaphysics of the moment. The fragile alliance between intellect and energy which characterized pop art at its finest has fallen prey to the very abstruseness pop began as a rebellion against. It is as though a great clown were to stop in the middle of his most hilarious routine, and offer us a soliloquy from

"Hamlet" while still in whiteface. The effect would be startling, but the true children in the audience would soon shift their attention to the center ring.

What is even more distressing has been the failure of pop to lead to anything. The movement has not even inspired its own antithesis. There is no anti-pop, no rejection of the superficial as a fit subject for investigation. Instead, the only signs of rebellion have been a widespread obliviousness to all that once made pop art seem dynamic. In music, the resurrection of rural verities (as represented in country and blues standards) is certainly an act of rebellion against the ethereal urbanity which now dominates rock. The old forms seem so unblemished, so incorruptible. "Progressive" rock has come to represent a vast compromise with the liberal establishment. I first realized during the Columbia revolt that hip radicals would eventually have to break with rock, because of its simple commitment to commercial success. During the "summer of love" that market value was viewed as evidence that the New Order was breaking through. But young activists have taught us all that the charts do not necessarily reflect genuine change, and in fact may actually indicate a preservation of the status-quo through its own determination to be flexible.

If rock is to retain its outcast's appeal, it must renounce its alliance with the intelligentsia. The simplest way of *seeming* to affect that renunciation is to declare the entire pop enlightenment null and void. Record companies investing in poeticized electropop are barking up the wrong amp. The last thing the underground wants from its music is an intellectual veneer. Nearly all the supergroups associated with "progressive" rock are withering on the vine. The Doors, for instance, have suffered an immense loss in prestige as a result of the disenchantment with "literate" pop. It is not that their music is any less exciting, nor can their decline be traced to any great change in their style. It is simply that the dynamic of enlightened theatricality which is so central to the experience of the Doors now seems ostentatious, even treacherous to their former fans. How cruel it must be to awake one morning and discover that you have metamorphosed overnight into a six-foot irrelevance.

But why stop with the Doors? The new Beatle album, as sturdy

and self-contained a package as they have ever released, has met with a mixed reception from hip critics on both sides of the Atlantic. The furor over those allegedly counter-revolutionary remarks is a convenient mask for those too righteous to admit that they have grown to distrust what they once embraced. Even if the Beatles had never expressed doubts about youthful insurrection, it would have been obvious from the tone of this new album that they are incapable of producing relevant art in a revolutionary context. Why should they be? The Beatles are "haves" in the most far-reaching sense of that word. They are the golden boys of pop, and we have no right to demand of them the consciousness of desperation which seems so appealing at the moment. To the Beatles, the entire upheaval which has so drastically altered the direction of youth culture throughout the western world must seem a simple matter of sexual impatience. "If you go carrying pictures of Chairman Mao/You ain't gonna make it with anyone anyhow" is the most honestly self-expressed couplet in any Beatles song to date. What is infuriating is the smug insularity those lines reflect. But that is inevitable if you happen to be a titan in a time when anti-heroes are chic.

In contrast, the new Rolling Stones album, *Beggar's Banquet,* has received unanimously favorable notices from the hip press. I don't deny its virtues. The arrangements are flawless, the tone subdued without seeming dull. But comparing *The Beatles* and *Beggar's Banquet* track by track, it is hard to imagine that anyone could condemn the Beatles and praise the Stones on technical grounds alone.

But the simple truth is that *Beggar's Banquet* is a far more relevant album than *The Beatles* and for that reason alone it is legitimate to call it the more satisfying work of art. The question of relevance is no critic's conceit—especially in rock, where it is the only truly relevant criterion. It is ironic that the Stones should grasp the importance of immediacy while the Beatles—who have always been so overtly concerned with the nuances of trend and taste—produce music that is oblivious to its time. Yet, the Stones have responded much more effectively to their audience's demand for songs that sound like rockabilly or blues. Their toast to "The

Salt of the Earth" is a calculated one, just as their re-working of a Bukkha White standard into "Prodigal Son" is a deliberate attempt to draw bonds between the blues revival and themselves.

The Beatles, on the other hand, seem more than ever the creatures of their own cosmology. Their new album relates more to the recent Hunter Davies biography than it does to the current pop scene. "It's gonna be all right," they croon at the end of *Revolution*. For them it probably will. But for the rest of us, those words delivered with such genial certainty, must seem as consoling as a tract on the glories of national pride written in 1939.

We much prefer the MC 5, and their open hostility to all that is "gentle" in rock. I only wish I could quote expressions, because the disdain expressed by their guitarist, Wayne Kramer, when the subject of psychedelic lightshows comes up, could easily fill an FBI file on subversive activity. As heroes of the new, down rock, the MC 5 reflect that distrust—so central to current youth culture—of the ornate, the educated, and the efficient. In America, it is inevitable that the rock underground must embrace the blues (just as French youth have renewed their interest in the traditional chanson) to maintain its position of seeming aesthetically "pure" without being intellectual. I don't mean to imply that the motives of white audiences in patronizing the blues are suspect because they spring from a desire to oppose the bourgeoisie. The question is relevance, not hypocrisy. How much more authentic Albert King seems, with his open-collar shirt, sipping orange juice between riffs, than Jim Morrison, who is all leather and lanolin. How much easier it is to adore Ma Rainey, who is black and rural-real, than Janis Joplin, who is white and nearly rich, and who comes from that latter-day Lourdes of dreams that dripped blood and money: San Francisco.

The rejection of mass-culture is a periodic occurrence in American life. It is certainly possible to compare the blues revival of 1968 with the folk renaissance of the early '60s. Both sprang from a similar disenchantment with the direction of pop music, and both reflected a deep yearning for simplicity, directness, and cultural authenticity. Even more important, both movements are at least causally related to a hostile political environment insensitive to the needs of the young. The folk revival, which achieved mass-

recognition during the New Frontier, was actually a product of the Eisenhower years. And the blues revival is the first cultural appointment of the Nixon administration.

What it signifies, essentially is a distrust of all innovation, when it is tied to popular appeal. The attitude of hip white audiences toward blues is essentially elitist. They are worshipping those delta gods to show their disdain for all who dig the Vanilla Fudge.

But in its allegiance to blues, the underground is actually functioning as an irredeemable part of the mass. The same distrust of "enlightened" culture can be felt in the mainstream of American life, as on its fringes. Is there anyone in this country—no matter what his taste—who has not been gravely disillusioned by the simple fact of existing in 1968? Isn't it inevitable that the violent changes we endured last year will result in a defensive suspicion of stylistic innovation? Can the electorate who chose Richard Nixon help but embrace the studied serenity Glenn Campbell represents? Can the good folks who buried Robert Kennedy resist the euphoria bubble gum music provides?

Actually the congruent rise of bubble gum music and the blues reflect the same basic tensions in American life. Both seek refuge from complexity and disunity in the power of pre-existent forms. B. B. King and the Ohio Express are both a great consolation to their audiences. A song like " Chewy, Chewy," with its essentially pornographic message delivered in an ingenuous vocal lilt, is in the great pop tradition of filth by association. "Do it to me baby, chew me out of my mind." I don't have the lyric sheet before me, but I think that's the final refrain. No less refreshing (for its conventionality as well as its implications) is "Cinnamon"; with an arched brow, one could interpret the refrain "Cinnamon/let me in" as the plaintive plea of a white boy (since that is obvious from the vocal) to a spicy black chick.

It is impossible to understand the blues revival without taking into consideration the sudden popularity of the conventional pop ballad. Topping the charts this week is "The Worst that Could Happen," a horrendously gaudy melodrama by the Brooklyn Bridge. It is significant that the Buddah label which recorded this track is also responsible for bubble gum music. Both trends represent a

commercial response to what Tin Pan Alley perceives as nostalgia for the tried and therefore true. Buddah has not ignored the blues. Their publicity campaign for the Barry Goldwater Reunion and for "Two Jews Blues" shows an awareness that white-blues and shlock rock are under the same causal umbrella.

The Scene, as I say, is looking stern these days. Upstairs, on 46th Street, they have opened up "the world's largest peep show," specializing in *those* magazines. If you look hard enough into the grimy window at 3 A.M. it becomes a Proustian mirror, reflecting the entire pop cosmos, which is truly the world's largest peep show.

Downstairs, amid the ruffles and the buckles and the faint aroma of olive oil shampoo, the view is even more prophetic. Three men are onstage, playing only two guitars and a set of drums. No gushing organ, no electric viola, not even a bass to provide the necessary electric guffaw. The drummer is unidentified, but superbly mellow. The guitarists are Slim Harpo and Lightnin' Slim. Delta to the tobacco stains. Slim Harpo keeps stealing these half-glances at the longhairs whirling around him, and if you watch closely, you can catch him cracking up behind his teeth.

The music is straight, pre-1948 Arhoolie blues, with just a lick of barroom jive and a hefty dose of country funk. It's as though none of that echo chamber ensemble effect had ever happened to the blues, as though it remained static—like on the radio—flash frozen so you could smell the imprisoned earth-aroma when you thawed it out. And all this was occurring amid the redbrick folds of Steve Paul's Scene, which is not so much a landmark as a symptom of New York pop music.

Astounding! In the audience, these four chicks are sitting around a votive candle left over from MacDougal Street in 1962; they're smoking and sipping and staring down a convenient crotch. And the one sheathed in voile, with spitcurls on her eyelashes—turns to her friend with the listing breasts, and sighs, "He really lays it down, that Lightnin' Slim." "Yeah," says the other. "Didn't he used to write for Cream?"

The moral is plain: aficionados would be advised to refrain from counting their chickens before they come home to roost. The blues revival is at best an interim, a necessary haven for pop refugees.

It will matter to the bulk of America only in its popularizers. The man who emerges from some cosmic delta to instant acclaim as a superstar will be the one who reconciles blues power with the freaky exhibitionism of rock. I'll wager a year's supply of Arhoolie records that he'll be a white man. Very white.

Maybe, even an albino.

—THE VILLAGE VOICE, 1968

# V
# HYPE

# AUTOHYPE: CONTEXT AS CRITERION

I first heard that term used by another rock critic, Robert Cristgau. We were sitting within shouting distance of each other at the Monterey Pop Festival, and I forgot who was burning whose guitar onstage while magic brownies made the rounds . . . but anyway, to the left of us stood a gaggle of men in double-breasted ecstasy, California breeze whistling through their razor cuts—that scene. And these men (who spend their days back in the city copulating with culture) were staring with the profundity of prophets at the crowd. A vast chorus of "groovy, groovy, oh wow, outasight!" arose from the arena, and these men heard the word. They knew then that a man may speak in signs, but dig his symbols and you've mastered his soul.

Ergo: autohype, the most dangerous form of flattery. You can autohype a woman, a revolution, a work of art. All publicity (political, sexual, and aesthetic) is aimed at getting you to convince yourself that the client in question should be canonized. Promotion is, more than anything, an art of self-suggestion. And I don't mean concentrated word of mouth. I mean the concerted effort to identify product with ethos and thus to render it sacred—above criticism. A good promo man is a mercantile shaman. Consider Saint Paul: he knew the value of a scene. He encouraged and supported the underground because he knew its existence was a most powerful instrument of autohype.

189

A scene makes judgment easy on the rest of us. It creates myth and market, aura and audience, product and prophecy. It accomplishes all this without ever stopping to think how little the dynamics of pushing have changed over the years. Old Paul never had to take his public out to lunch.

How do autohypnotists cultivate and manipulate the pop scene? First, they talk in tongues (fostering miracle, mystery, and authority, like the Grand Inquisitor). They offer group warmth ("We're all so beautiful here in Max's Plastic Epiphany. We're young and special and this album turns us on this month"). Finally, they traffic in bogus payola, disguised as revelation ("Jimi Hendrix —you dig—is black!").

The successful para-publicist can shield any work or dogma from the barbs of pragmatic criticism, which strives to consider each event in terms of its own expectations. One sign of autohype: today's rock audience is terribly eager to render *a priori* praise. If the underground did not exist, folks, the company freaks would have to invent it.

Publicity men seldom sweat their clients' bad notices. They know it's the mention, not the verdict, that sells product. Besides, making judgments is parental and no critic can afford to be over thirty today. Instead of dissecting, critics rap. Watch for this tendency to avoid confrontation: it is more pronounced among rock critics, not because we are a younger lot, but because we have been suckled by the brain police from birth. There are many ways to avoid confrontation in a rock review. Be cryptic. Talk about getting high. Mention the revolution. Quote Plato. Do your thing. All these copouts say something: they say the critic is afraid to evaluate.

A critic doesn't tell us what is good or bad anymore. He merely puts the pieces in perspective. As an impressionist in an age of impressions (we strive to know what we feel) he has become a farmer of his own perceptions, yielding a crop of emotions which, when harvested between margins, becomes an opinion. In a favorable ("up") review, he recounts his own shock of recognition. To call something bad art, he recollects his own boredom. Somehow, to do otherwise today—insisting upon the possibility of absolute success or failure—is to run the risk of sounding like a college

instructor and not a critic. There is something academic about a man who looks at art today and claims to know.

Perhaps that is inevitable in an age when men are likely to mutter "absurd" the way they once said "dammit." But I think the temptation to eulogize one's immediate reactions—to groove—is one reason why context is so important in all the pop arts, and especially in rock.

At the risk of sounding personal, I suggest that this elevation of context to the level of critierion is much more than a critic's hang-up. I have no empirical evidence, but only a haunting suspicion that my writing elicits a more sympathetic response when it deals with approach than when it attempts to define stands. If this is fact as well as paranoia, then the creator—who, after all has a far greater stake in achieving approval than I do—must feel an irresistible urge to stake out his territory and only as an afterthought to fill it. In pop music, which is only slightly less ephemeral than journalism, that urge must be an instinct. Go home, kid, and find yourself a bag.

So Donovan comes on like a gypsy botanica. So Jimi Hendrix goes to England, learns to come in colors, and emotes like a motherfucker. So the Vanilla Fudge sing Beethoven. So Tom Jones dabbles in plastic macho. So Judy Collins sings a Ballata of Francesco Landini which could have put Jesus to sleep on the cross. So the Stones twang, the Who sell out, and the Beatles shed their skins seasonally, like lizards.

Style is of primal importance for the pop creator. His job is no longer the communication of a culture (we call that Socialist Realism and sneer) or even communication of self (that died when the underground replaced Dale Carnegie as the arbiter of influence). Today's artist communicates a context. He arrives prepackaged and it is the critic's job to give him a brand name. The most significant thing in rock today is motif. A total concept sells records. Ask the Beatles how context protects and personifies ("Nothing you can speak which can't be chic").

I often wonder why a skillful group soon sounds stale unless its presentation evolves. I think the answer lies in our own expectations from art. We want it to pose. Substance doesn't intrigue us, but we react to style. And we have robbed the critic of what used

to constitute his most important function—telling the difference between the two. Both, we exult, are the same.

I mean these columns to function as a survival manual for pop fans. Rock is an ecstatic business; learn to distill its energy and don't waste strength on hype, unless you're into that. Two years ago, I wrote in one of my first columns that rock needed a critic. Now I think it needs a shit-detector. Someone who can stand up to the Grand Inquisitor, in his expense-account halo, and ask him why miracle, mystery, and authority are more important for a rock group than soul.

—THE VILLAGE VOICE, 1968

# ● MOVER

"How many columns you get in *Newsweek?*"

Even over the phone, he kisses, then slaps, you with his voice. Hit-and-run chatter bristles across the wires. You are taking notes, trying to see the trap before it forms.

"They use photos?"

"Yep."

"How many columns did your picture take up?"

"One."

Dazzling. The moment of super-suave. You listen to his voice rear back in triumph, the gentle cough before the words meant to jolt you, jab you, make you bleed. Then—fast, like a matador:

"Mine took two. They loved me."

Olé. He grabs the ears and tail and departs to win at something else. He'll call again tomorrow, twice. Once to read you his column from *Nightbeat* (which sounds like three of his phone calls stripped of yawns and pauses) and once to bawl you out for staying away from his club last night, when it was all absolutely happening, positively, man.

Last year, Steve Paul owned Manhattan's most envied discotheque, the Scene. His club sprawled over the cellar of a West Side building like the amorphous arms of some massive sewage system. The place was full of corners; you could always find privacy in all that public.

193

Steve Paul's knack for spotlighting unbroken acts amid all that nightglow musk made the show erratic but exciting. But the lines stretching onto Eighth Avenue every night weren't filled with searchers after talent. Steve Paul could have set a block of limp cheese onstage to rot in the spotlight, and not many customers would have noticed. It is to his credit that his entertainment was live and breathing.

The Scene was its own attraction. Nightly to a wall-to-wall audience, it acknowledged applause from hands limp with reputation. It accepted ebullient nods from celebrities and hippie praise from show-biz extras who spent their unwinding hours on the dance floor. It grew known, renowned, and In.

Steve Paul got his picture in a lot of papers. *Newsweek* chronicled "the sad demise of the Stork Club and the explosive emergence of the Scene" in one week. *The New York Times* contributed five columns of newsprint and three photo layouts. Society columnists made the club their salon-of-the-moment, Tennessee Williams met his understudies over frug and frenzy. Sammy Davis, Jr. sang for free and the eggplant starlets screamed. The Great Discovery happened: another plebeian palace ready to be plucked by the withered, with-it overworld. The kids left for anonymous clubs on the East Side, but the Jet Set made the scuffed dance floor the ground whereon aristocrats tried to look good dancing.

Steve Paul poured on the sauce. He was his own cook, dishwasher, and maître d'. He handled these jobs with a deftness that stunned. His club was the real thing—a controlled slum, the kind that doesn't knife you if you walk through at 4 A.M. So everyman who was anybody showed up to sit in a corner. And Steve Paul became a slumlord with soul.

> The Scene was THE club in New York in the true sense and the business sense and the hip sense and the decency sense.
> We aimed at happenings in a nonstructured way. Nothing happened, but things occurred from time to time.
> There was no differentiation in terms of structure between audience, staff, and entertainers.
> There was a certain honesty and decency and creativity, so naturally it was special.

It was a tremendously secure world of nightly occurrence. Everybody was like turned-on and jumping around with the club, and I would like to go into the back room and cry.

Steve Paul is one light year older now. His reputation lies strewn across a couch, a cornucopia yellowing at the corners.

In a *Journal-American* article calling him the "folk-rock philosopher," he admits "Of course, sex plays an important part in discotheque dancing." He displays two columns by Dick Schaap, side by side. One is a put-up, one a put-down. He loves both. Someone calls his club a "murky, mad cellar." He chuckles over "my hippest piece of publicity," an article by Pete Hamill which accuses him of being "part of the lie that it is more important to be hip than good."

"You're in the center, man, when you're mentioned in other people's columns," he says. "If they're old women reporters from the *Times,* I'm a nice kid. And when they call me 'a 23-year-old tormented genius,' I know I reacted groovy enough. Truth and groove win out, right man?"

Steve Paul is the Jack Paar of rock. He doesn't sing or dance or tell funny stories. He brings it all together. This is hard work with lousy hours. The only fringe benefit is fame. So Steve Paul stands in the door of his club drinking in the crowd, searching for FACES among the coats and hats.

As emcee, he sometimes sits at the feet of his entertainers. No one has actually seen him cry onstage, but he claims he has for so long that everyone believe it. It's part of the cool.

"He's all wrapped up in ego like an onion, and when you peel the layers away, it just collapses."

"He likes people with reputation. He's got a certain knack—a sense of proportion. It's uncanny he's still around."

"He's really rather inarticulate. When I came to condense what he was saying, I couldn't. He was using lots of words, but he was still nonverbal."

"He's a mess who moves things."

His house is four stories high; each room is a compact floor with a fireplace. Telephones bridge all the gaps; extensions twinkle like Christmas lights. When the phone rings, it gongs,

He lives on the ragged edge of the Village in a townhouse. His

block looks like the bottom of a chestnut vendor's barrel—with soot from warehouses, grease from all-night diners, and fog that creeps across the river and down the street.

Inside is the Scene without spotlights. Each room is tastefully overdecorated in Michael Malcé modern. Walls of exposed brick are bathed in murky half-light. A large window of leaded glass illustrates the bedroom. The refrigerator is covered with wood-tone Contac.

"I refurbished this place by adding myself," your host offers, watching to see that written down. Making good copy is something he learned at seventeen, when he was a public relations man. Interviewing Steve Paul is like watching an ugly girl do the dance of the seven veils—the anticipation is not about what's underneath but over whether it's worth the wait.

You get a tour, an offer of Coke and a cigarette, and the chance of confrontation. There is veil number one before you: Stevie-baby the PR man, churning out copy. "The Scene is part of the continuing search for me to express myself," he begins, waiting tastefully until the words register. "I have no throne and I feel sorry for my pretenders because it doesn't exist. I'm in competition with nobody." Get all that, his eyes ask? "It takes me to be me. I fill my role pretty well."

His delivery of Paulisms—those epigrammatic gems that go nowhere but look great—is flawless. What do you want in an idol, Steve? "Myself plus one." In a girl? "Herself plus one." A friend? "An equal."

If you let him, Steve Paul gives a write-it-yourself interview. He drops the pieces one by one into your lap and they assemble themselves into the image of a corduroy celebrity.

"I gave away two thousand buttons of paintings because of my feeling that art should be extended everywhere till people understand that art is life and life is art. No promotion, just for the groove of it." Veil number two: Steve the Artiste, the stage-struck savant. He does the dogma soft-shoe like a real philosophe. "There are two realities: the world of universal reality (which is the ability to achieve what you want from the social machinery) and the world of personal reality (which is your emotions). To exist in one or

the other is to exist in nothing. The only thing that matters is to be in the world of spiritual reality, which is synthesis."

Veil three: Steve the celebrity. A chance guest shot on the "Les Crane Show" brought him a flood of letters and a show of his own. "I was the hottest thing in America," he recalls. "All those columns, all that space—you're a journalist, do you realize what that means? I was the subject of TV profiles in Italy and Germany."

Paul's first TV show turned out to be an autobiography looking for its subject. It was also his last. His mistake then, as always, was playing mind over material. The publicity too came and went, and not long after the demise of the TV show, the Scene began to flounder; then it sank. The Jet Set took off with as much noise as it had made in landing, and the click of high heels became an empty echo on Steve Paul's dance floor. Gross went down to one third of peak. Paul refuses to blame the club's decline on the rise of nouveau-chic discos along the Third Avenue axis, or the departure of those searchers after plebe-rock to the real slum on the Lower East Side. He says: "We were busy being busy instead of grooving. It was a matter of repeating spontaneity."

Steve Paul must have spent a few memorable nights in his town-house during his downfall. But he never acknowledges depression. Veil number four has "I am an achiever-believer" written all over it. The solution to decline is reconstruction. Steve Paul is now en-gaged, with all the naked want of a master builder, in renovating the Scene into a hip Disneyland, with a stellar cast from the avant-garde freaking freely over the same crags and crannies the celebs used to chic in. With his uncanny ability to build gigs—to bring the singer and the song together in his club—he has constructed an impressive lineup: the Blues Project, Muddy Waters, the Rascals, and Tim Hardin in his first New York engagement. Allen Ginsberg is slated to lead audiences in singing chants and mantras. Steve Paul is opening his club to a new kind of aristocracy, the plastic galaxy of the New Bohemia. If he fails, everyone will say the idea was pretentious all along. If he succeeds, Steve Paul will be the Sol Hurok of the avant-garde, importing attractions from the East Village, the Strip, the Bay Shore Area, and beyond.

That role demands more than a critic's vision and a businessman's

agility. Being a hustler isn't enough; you've got to be a hip messiah. Steve Paul wants to be the saver and the saved.

"If one person—ME—can turn on Bob Dylan and *Newsweek* in one week, and get Allen Ginsberg and Murray the K to donate their services, he would have to be, at the least, not a bad person, and a success," he reasons. The code of the mover: product is all. Currently, product is the Velvet Underground, belting spectral atonality while Andy Warhol programs an "underground amateur hour." A mod wedding with a guru officiating is in the offing, and Paul is thinking of holding onstage auditions for the lucky couple. The underground has already met Tin Pan Alley. At the Scene, it will touch Seventh Avenue. When you're cooking with chic, anything is possible, even soi-disant friendship with Andy Warhol. "First we met to exploit each other," Paul explains. "Then for whatever we can do for each other. And then as people who appreciate the aspects of tragedy and absurdity of our times."

Such rapport notwithstanding, Warhol's Velvet Underground needed a sounding board, and the Scene is providing a productive partnership. Murray the K's connection with Steve Paul is more symbiotic than charismatic. Tim Hardin is appearing at the Scene with love and a hefty advance from its owner. Steve says top groups take severe cuts in pay because "they want to save this place and make it live again." But his claim that the Young Rascals worked two nights for peanuts is disputed by their manager who says: "They got gate money and Steve took in from the bar. Sure the Rascals like him, but they have management and they have bills to pay." Both or none of these versions may be true.

Steve Paul is a damned good mover. But the role is too spurious for him to accept. His assessment of the qualities needed to stay on top ("personality in contrast to love and niceness") shows a slashing pragmatic thrust. He flaunts his accomplishments with the grace of a man proud of success ("I wanted a TV show—even if it was a bad one—and I got it; I wanted the hippest club in New York and now I've got that").

But Steve Paul's life is a William Burroughs truism: "Selling is more of a habit than using." Steve Paul Associates handled publicity for the Peppermint Lounge before its founder was old enough to drink there. Steve Paul speculated on the stock market as an

adolescent. Steve Paul dropped out of Dobbs Ferry, took refuge from N.Y.U., and lived in everything from a room at the Y to a penthouse down the block.

But he resents all those hustler accomplishments because that isn't hip. "Until I was nineteen or twenty, I was completely full of shit. I felt uncomfortable being full of shit," he says uncomfortably. "I was concerned with power for power's sake, and money for money's sake."

Now Steve Paul Associates handles one client. More veils slide off as he loses his cool. He switches masks on command, getting stoned on what he takes to be a lack of sympathy. You can see it in the corners of his eyes—my god, this guy is writing a piece on me, and he doesn't dig me—he really doesn't dig me. Steve Paul almost cries.

The whole thing takes ten minutes. Veil five—the hippie put-down—slips off seductively. Veil six—at least I'm honest—wriggles free. And now it is down to underthings: Steve Paul the mixed-up kid. In his kitchen, he scrapes the walls of his ego in search of material—always new material.

"See, when I was a kid I used to lie and steal." He licks his lips hopefully. "I mean I used to . . . I had a modicum of success and I used to stretch it. I stole from my mother. See, there was this bureau; I still remember it. There were three drawers and the one on the right was verboten. I used to cop quarters and things."

The saga continues: "When I was older, I'd steal from my roommate, go out and spend $6 on food and say it cost nine, you owe me $4.50—a million things like that in a million different ways."

His eyes stop moving for the first time that evening. His pupils stand dead still. "I just stopped it . . . really . . . first the big lies and then the little ones . . . then everything. And now, what hangs me up man . . . wow . . . I tell the truth and still think I'm lying. I have to tell myself, hey stop telling all that, and then I realize . . . man, it's all really happening. It is a strange thing . . . wow, very strange."

Steve Paul works his balls off to make the Scene work. It's a good club, sometimes great, not because he stands onstage sobbing solipsistic epiphanies to an audience that gobs on his soul, but despite it. It's got good acts, not because Steve Paul can move

mountains, but because he knows how to use money wisely and well. It will probably succeed, not because a man can will a movement but because the underground needs a springboard in midtown.

But Steve Paul won't let the mover in him ply his trade in peace. There is a certain beauty in the pure act of hustling, in Steve Paul's own kid dream of "meaning no evil but not being especially hung up on the good." But he will never appreciate his own aesthetic. Instead he walks a line between hustling and grooving. He tries, by his own definition, "to worm my way in without being wormy."

He succeeds where it shows. He fills his empty house with phone calls. He marshals Andy Warhol's people together like a den mother ("Andy's at the Stalls? I mean, the Sculls? Well, get him over to the club; the New York *Post* wants to do a photo layout. C'mon, you've gotta move"). His chest expands over the phone, his legs cross languidly.

On the radio, Murray the K is interviewing Tim Hardin. More good works. Steve Paul got these men together. An hour before, when Murray called complaining that Hardin was late, Steve explained about artists and obligation and poetic license. When he listens to the interview actually happening, he beams, and shakes his head, and chuckles: "Wow." It is natural because Steve Paul feels real when he moves things.

—The Village Voice, 1966

# MASTER OF MEDIOCRITY

Way back there—in 1952—WFIL-TV in Philadelphia had a hassle on its hands. The disc jockey-host of its popular daytime "Bandstand" show had been charged with participating in "improper activities." That was a key phrase of the fifties. Just its utterance in tocsin tones, or its appearance in erect black headlines brought a not unpleasant chill to the nation's collective spine. Mouths salivated, ears perked up, and eyes read on.

Lest anybody wonder what sort of "improper activities" this broadcaster had indulged in, the authorities were holding in abeyance a member or two of the show's teen-age regulars, FEMALES! It was, in short, the kind of scandal everyone loved in those days— a vaguely plausible one.

As the story broke, WFIL found itself in the same boiling water that was later to solidify everything diverse in America into a hardboiled egg. The station's brass scanned the industry for a replacement. They were looking for someone with a face like Bromo-Seltzer, whose very appearance would neutralize the doubts parents everywhere felt about their kids and their times. They wanted someone who could project, with utter certainty, the spinach culture of the fifties: it was hard to swallow, but good for you.

They found him on television, in Utica, New York. He had already made the big jump from a nearby radio station where he hosted a seven hour daily dose of pop music. He was—as one

reporter later attested—"a solidly built square-shouldered lad, with an Arrow-collar profile and a deep portentious voice." There were no skeletons in his split-level closet, just a lot of two-button jackets and ties. At five, he had published a neighborhood gossip sheet; at six, he owned a sidewalk peanut-butter restaurant. President of his high-school class, he sold brushes door to door and built chicken crates at 52 cents an hour in college. His classmates at Syracuse University voted him "the man most likely to sell the Brooklyn Bridge."

Richard Augustus Clark II almost did!

They loved him from the start at WFIL. "To many mothers," wrote one copybopper, "the afternoon show has brought a sudden closer relationship with their children. 'He's sort of a big brother who sets a good example,' one father commented. 'Since Bandstand, kids have insisted on wearing jackets and girls have cooled it on too-tight sweaters.' Parents applauded."

So did the rating services. Shortly after Clark took over, Philadelphia's Bandstand became the highest-rated pre-dinner TV program in any major American city. Before you could say "Better buy Bird's Eye," the show was syndicated over the ABC network. At its peak, "American Bandstand" ran on 105 stations, reaching over 20 million teenagers. It became a springboard for variations on the stiffly stylized rite of adolescent dancing; it nurtured the Calypso, the Circle, the Stroll, and a bouffant ballet known in lingua franca as "Phillie style." It rocketed the southside Italian ghetto-dubbed "Brotherlylovesville" by the promo men—into national prominence. Superstars sat on their stoops combing their pompadours and waiting to be found. Under the knowing aegis of Dick Clark's associate, Bob Marcucci, they sometimes were.

Fabian (né Fabian Forte) was discovered at a record hop; he walked in and all the girls started screaming. "That was enough for us," explains Clark. "You don't look for a singer. The person who is the star has that magic thing, and that's all that matters. Fabian was always a far better actor than anything else."

In his leopard-skin shirt, very open at the throat, Fabian appeared on "American Bandstand" to grunt songs like "Tiger" and "Turn Me Loose." He was an echo-chamber Frankenstein, created in the recording studio. On TV, he merely mouthed the words to pre-

recorded tracks. That Fabian couldn't sing was irrelevant; he worked in an image medium, and his audience squealed with a special delight when he fluffed his lines. Informality and ecstasy, the two pillars of teen culture in the fifties, had little to do with synchronization.

"American Bandstand" made superstars of a galaxy of tousled crooners from South Philadelphia, who dropped a few vowels from their names in a gesture of showbiz Americanization, and went on as Connie Francis, Frankie Avalon, or Bobby Rydell. While they sang or signed autographs, the Bandstand regulars strolled, bopped, and went steady. Their look was copied verbatim and Clark delighted in displaying a bulletin board filled with photos of studied look-alikes. That was the kind of rapport Bandstand thrived on. For the first time, after-school America was experiencing instant identity.

Books away and televisions on, they danced under the klieg lights or clapped their hands hypnotically. "We like Beechnut spearmint gum," they chanted in unison, fingering beads and badges inscribed with the holy word "IFIC." A skinny kid in a sequin-speckled suit bellowed into a dead mike; he looked like a cheap engagement ring but everyone screamed anyway. Old folks, busy conforming, called it "conformity." But a viable, visible sub-culture had been born on "American Bandstand" and Dick Clark—the guy in the plastic surgeon's mask—had shown us how easy a delivery it could be.

"I don't make culture," he insists today. "I sell it. A myth has grown up over the years that I have something to do with what becomes popular. Generally, I reflect what's going on early enough to make a profit on it. It's not my business to interpret."

He sits in a comfortably padded chair in his office on Sunset Boulevard. It is fifteen years after Dick Clark first climbed on the Bandstand bandwagon and over 2500 miles from Brotherlylovesville. He is pudgier now around the cheeks. There are off-camera wrinkles above his brow. But he still speaks like a disc jockey; in conversation, he announces each idea as though it were a new record. He seems to be wearing the same necktie he has used every day of his career. But he has worn the two-button wash-and-wear

uniform well, and he is not about to part with it. All that distinguishes Dick Clark from the nice-guy mold are his fingernails—cut and polished to perfection. But who can deny a successful guy his manicure?

"I'm getting older and wiser, but I stay the same," he says. "My clothing changes according to the style for my age, but my relationship with kids doesn't. I was too old then to be a playmate, and too young to be a father. It's still that way. I'm constantly called upon to explain kids. It's a peculiar thing for me because I don't make believe I'm a kid. I'm an observer and a presenter." His eyes twinkle like a busy switchboard. "I've made a career out of being non-controversial."

Dick Clark gives an interview the way he runs his career. Everything he says is instantly screened. Opinions are followed by the inevitable warning, "You'd better not quote me on that." He is especially wary of the press. "People who write use me as a scapegoat," he confides.

Not always. When Clark first joined the panoply of television's host-celebrities, the fourth estate had nothing but praise. "He has become a symbol for all that is good in America's younger generation," burbled one writer. "Dick's acts of kindness are a legend," chortled another.

Legend they truly were. As the first man to achieve a nationwide audience of doting, solvent teenagers, Clark was the virtual dictator of Tin Pan Alley in 1959. While his patronage did not assure a hit, it helped many a gold record along the way. "When I recorded 'Venus,'" singer Frankie Avalon told one interviewer, "Dick got behind it and it sold 1.5 million copies. He's the greatest."

Frankie Avalon was not the only one to stand in awe. A congressional sub-committee then involved in probing graft within the record industry soon took a lively interest in Dick Clark's enterprises. To put it as tactfully as Richard Augustus II himself would, he was suspected of confusing aesthetic with financial judgment. In fact, it was not long after Frankie Avalon's tribute appeared that Rep. Peter F. Mack of Illinois called Clark "Top dog in the payola field."

With a press turned gleefully hostile, Dick Clark entered the halls of Congress to testify. As the Associated Press described it

on April 29, 1960: "Dick Clark suavely swore today that his
hands were never dirtied by payola." Soberly, he insisted his invest-
ments were neither improper nor uncommon, and staunchly accepted an ultimatum from ABC to divest himself of all outside
interests. With a little soap and water behind the ears, Dick Clark
was clean.

America acquitted, or at least forgave, Dick Clark. True, he was
no longer the white knight riding off into a kinescopic sunset. But
the scandals of the fifties had taught us not to demand propriety
from our leaders, only cleverness and poise.

Dick Clark's calculated cool helped him survive. He developed a
tough, arrogant honesty about his work. His interviews were
peppered with knowing asides. "I don't think Hollywood knows
any kids," he told the Los Angeles *Times,* "because, by the time
they get here, they aren't kids anymore." When asked why he had
decided to return to television as a dramatic actor, he forsook the
stock answer about art and fulfillment, and quipped, "I decided if
I wanted people to continue knowing who I am, I'd better figure
out how many different ways I can poke my face on TV." And he
added without a trace of the bashful elan which once accompanied
such observations: "I always seem to play the nice, clean-cut fellow
who turns out to be a louse."

Like Richard Nixon, Dick Clark had realized that the only
humility we require from the defeated is pragmatism. We are able
to accept idealism only from a winner. All-American boys who
tarnish soon find themselves coming on as though innocence were
a kind of virginity they have lost long ago, in some brothel of the
soul. No longer quite clean-cut, Dick Clark's dignity had become
that of the successful entrepreneur. It was his only remaining claim
to grace and he has lived off it ever since.

He is anything but washed up today. Though he never left the
periphery of the scene, there are signs that he is inching toward
its center again. He says he has moved to Los Angeles because it is
"the most youth-oriented city in the nation," and his camera crews
can be seen canvassing the freeways and taco stands in search of
the Now. Not long ago the Los Angeles *Free Press* discovered
Clark's pop-squad shooting a film called *"Love in Haight."* If the

hippy thing fails, there is always Country-Western music. (Clark owns a station and produces a show called "Swinging Country.") With the perennial success of patriotic monologues on records, Clark has a new single called "Open Letter To the Older Generation." And his partner of long standing, Bob Marcucci, is re-activating the old Chancellor label, which once showcased the brightest bellowers of "American Bandstand." To mark its grand re-entry, Marcucci plans to introduce a new singer from old South Philadelphia called Bobby Jason. He makes his recording debut with an updated version of "Venus," the song Dick Clark once helped Frankie Avalon sell a million and a half copies of.

If Bobby Jason clicks, Clark can do it again. His production company is one of those showbiz complexes geared to thrive behind pasteboard properties. From a carpeted cottage on Sunset Boulevard, Clark runs the largest personal-appearance packaging agency in the world (it employs a staff of 40 and handles upwards of 300 one-night stands a year). Right now, its most important clients are the Monkees. Their association with Dick Clark seems inevitable. His genius has always been making gravy from raw meat, and convincing a hungry public that his gruel is healthier than the real thing.

"The name of the game is show business," Clark shrugs. His clients always play it well. The Monkees dab honesty make-up on their faces, and come on real. They wear musicianship like a tiara. "Their show is full of exuberance," Clark insists. "They do four or five costume changes, and it lasts a full hour. They don't do a fast fifteen minutes like our British friends."

Few subjects provoke as carping a response from Dick Clark as the English rock invasion. No wonder; what finally ended his pop dictatorship was not scandal or boredom, but the Beatles, with a little help from their friends. Though Clark goes easy on the Beatles ("Their major accomplishment," he thinks, "was getting the older generation interested in rock,") he calls the folk-rockers who followed them "the greatest danger to pop music." What he objects to most is their repudiation of show business. "They get so involved in being admired by the people around them," he explains, "that they forget about the audience."

Clark's emphasis on commercialism (the audience first!) is un-

derstandable; he reigned in the age of the pop professional, who fit his personality to the function at hand. But the Beatles ushered in an era of the musician-idol, who sang and spoke his own thoughts. They were the first to prove that a rock performer could be his own image-maker. In the fifties, folk-rock singers Simon and Garfunkel found it necessary to call themselves Tom and Jerry, and act accordingly. But after the Beatles, they used their own names, and made it—as they felt it.

This new naturalness dethroned Dick Clark. The folk-rockers were amateurs in a sense which must have enraged him; they emphasized individuality over role, making their style impossible to assemble as a pop commodity. Dick Clark could create a celebrity, but not a Bob Dylan.

In 1965, with a galaxy of rock subversives carving up the world into fan clubs, Clark found himself in the same kind of situation that had spawned him ten years before. Rock 'n' roll was again a puzzling, even threatening, phenomenon to adults—so hairy that they sometimes had it banned. It is no accident that the Beatles and the Rolling Stones began in conscious imitation of pre-Bandstand rock idols whose black-and-blue sweat-music turned kids on and put adults uptight.

In the mid-fifties, teenagers occupied a prominent place in the headlines as hoodlums-saints not fit to be seen below the waist. The teen-hero had a lean and hungry look. His hair curled down over the bridge of his nose like a Sicilian grape arbor. His motorcycle jacket glittered with the reflected glory of a hundred brass studs. His parents thought he was a killer, but his girl knew he was a rebel without a cause, oppressed from all sides. If James Dean brought the teenage ethos of rumbling, bumbling sensuality to the screen, the hit parade was filled with its musical extensions: a yielding, yearning ecstasy that was almost antithetical to the Mickey Spillane adult culture of the time.

Dick Clark made his mark by castrating this teen hero. He substituted romance for sex, neckties for leather jackets, and swirling dance-curlicues for grinding. His music—with its Little League lushness—was acepted by adults as bad, but safe. Nobody ever banned Frankie Avalon. Even the fuzz approved. Said one

official of the New York Police Department, "Dick Clark acts as a tranquilizing pill on youngsters."

He has been offering the same musical Miltown ever since. In the post-Bandstand years, his clients have maintained an uncanny sameness. Even when longhaired, they are happy, reverent kids with watermelon eyes and cantaloupe voices. Like Paul Revere and the Raiders, a creampuff combo Clark found in the Pacific Northwest, they are costumed players, calculated to reassure everyone that the kids are all right (i.e. obedient.)

For awhile, repeated exposure on a daily pre-taped Clark package called "Where The Action Is" helped to establish the Raiders. In tight, taut britches and Revolutionary War frock coats which never hid their thighs, they romped and bounded past the cameras like the Three Stooges in Colonial drag. An early anti-drug sermon called "Kicks" brought them to the attention of disc jockeys during a spate of baffling psychedelic-code-songs. By once more exploiting the fears of adults, Dick Clark tried to sell the Raiders to the young as their own.

"We almost made it that time," he reflects today. But with the cancellation of "Where The Action Is," the group has all but faded, except on the vanity tables of pre-teens where they remain enshrined. Clark's other "Action" properties have met similar fates; we will probably never again get a chance to worship at the feet of Keith Allison (who was discovered when he happened by an "Action" set only because he looked like Paul McCartney. "Later," Clark explains, "we found out he could sing").

Later, we found out he couldn't!

Can Dick Clark do it again? Will we commission him to perform another hysterectomy? His scalpel is raised, his anesthesia ready for admission whenever we choose to breathe. If he does succeed in 1968, it will be because we need him. Dick Clark is a master of mediocrity, and Americans have a strange affection for the banal. It shows most during times of stress. In the prime spinach-years of "American Bandstand," we were all afraid of excellence. We wanted, more than anything, to be alike. Today, when that sameness had been smashed, we wonder if the center can hold together

at all. If it cannot, Dick Clark will emerge in every field from pop to politics.

He leans back in his leather chair, feet firmly planted in California carpeting, and observes, "I'm one of the world's great finger-pointers." Then, with the grace of a man who knows when to be modest, he adds, "You'd better not quote me on that."

—WEST MAGAZINE, 1968

# ● 69 WITH A BULLET

Every morning after his coffee break, he looks up from his over-sized teakwood desk, plows through a snowdrift of unread releases, opens the intercom, and asks Shirley for the advance charts. She skips in dutifully a few minutes later and presents him with a freshly-Xeroxed tearsheet. Today it is the *Billboard* chart, in advance of publication. His eyes admit an expanse of print, but his mind focuses on one line.

He's the president of an "indie" record company, so tiny the landlord keeps a moving van in the alley, so shaky the floor wobbles every time one of his seven records drops a point on the charts.

He runs his eyes over the Xerox copy and jubilantly phones his wife out in Great Neck. Through the sound of a distant soap opera, he shouts defiantly: "It's number 69 with a bullet."

A bullet (appropriately colored blood red) is a small dot superimposed upon the rating number of a pop single. It means a sudden leap in salability. The bouncing red dot is a major factor in the engineering of a hit record. It makes the shops triple their orders. It makes the DJs in San Antonio sit up and take notice. It's the best way to break into airplay lists in major markets like Chicago, Los Angeles, and especially New York.

Most AM pop stations are straight-jacketed into a top-25 format. It's not unusual to hear only 12 records in an hour, between commercials, station jingles, newscasts, DJ-vaudeville routines, give-

210

aways, editorials, and "public service" announcements. This tight format makes experimentation impossible and the charts crucial. Outside of an occasional golden-oldie, there is almost nothing to play but chart. On rare occasions when an AM station devotes three minutes to a new single, it usually does so because of those red dots.

Their justification is that the bullets signify nationwide popularity. Single records are seldom released nationally. They are tested, like any new product, on "selected" markets. This means a song like "Bang Bang," by the Joe Cuba Sextet, gets a trial run in strong Latin American markets like the barrios of New York. While the song is a smash on local stations, it has barely started to move on the national charts. But with the ghettos under its belt, the company goes all-out for coast-to-coast saturation.

A new psychedelic sound may be broken first in the San Francisco Bay area, the theory being if it doesn't sell in home territory, forget it. Or an urban folk-rock singer may find his record on trial in Tallahassee because, if they buy it in the boondocks, they'll eat it with a spoon in Greenwich Village.

The aim, in all cases, is not so much to sell records as to prove potential salability. Our promo-man aims to convince disc jockeys that they can't program pop music without including his song in their play lists. He probably won't succeed by delivering this pitch over lunch at the Colony. But he knows that every disc jockey and program director worth his five-digits reads charts with a beady pupil set diligently on those little red bullets.

It sounds fair because the charts are supposed to indicate which records the public is buying. But it doesn't necessarily work that way, because the most important factor in the rise of a hit record is radio airplay. *Billboard* and *Cashbox* study the airplay sheets of pop radio stations all over the nation. What classifies a record as rhythm and blues is not the Negritude of the singer, but the fact that self-designated R and B stations are playing it. A country-western or "easy listening" release is so-called because radio stations consider it that. When "easy listening" (lushly orchestrated ballad) releases make the charts, as they do today, it means that key stations are pushing soft music in preference to so-called "hard" rock. This,

of course, is what is happening on stations all over the country which follow trends like bloodhounds.

The power of the New York disc jockey over the records you hear is reflected in the *Billboard* Hot 100. The number one record in the nation is not necessarily the record people are buying most; it's the record disc jockeys are playing most often. A popular song may never rise on the charts if disc jockeys refuse to play it. Stations with the greatest percentage of "breakout" records are not in New York or Chicago. In fact, top-25 stations in big markets are usually unwilling to break new records. They prefer to watch consumer response to a new disc as it is broken in select rural areas or small cities. This means that the records you hear and the music your dealer stocks have been previously chosen by disc jockeys in the hinterlands. No major city has a breakout station on AM radio— only obedient echoes.

The de-selection of controversial music from the Hot 100 is such a pervasive reality that the folk-rock genre is fast becoming a music played only on special "underground" stations. In fact, the success of the rock underground proves something unique about the new sound; it spreads through word-of-mouth. Folk-rock hits move from campus to discotheque, eventually working their way into the pop mainstream through the underground press. Groups like Country Joe and the Fish and the Paul Butterfield Blues Band never made the *Billboard* charts with singles, but they command rapt audiences in city rock clubs, where fans come to listen, not to dance.

There is no such thing as a separate underground listing but perceptive chart-gazers are already predicting the appearance of such a survey soon. What would follow then, one envisions, is the birth of underground radio, geared toward a young urban audience and reflecting a large collegiate market. There are already such hip-rock stations on many campuses and West Coast hard-rock outlets are the first to learn not to limit themselves to the top 25.

But the New York AM scene remains shackled to the red bullets. WMCA says it bases its own top 25 on listener response, jukebox plays, and record sales. But, says one official: "The top 25 is our view of the most popularly listened-to records. It's qualitative as well as quantitative."

What he means is that WMCA charts the most popular records

it is playing—not necessarily the most popular records on the market. The sudden disappearance of a song like "They're Coming to Take Me Away, Ha-Ha" from the charts does not mean people have stopped buying the song. On the contrary, if the effect of censorship on book sales and film gross is any guide, Napoleon XIV must have made a bundle. But, since WMCA does not always reflect true popular taste on its charts, we will never know how the song sold.

The new Troggs release, "I Can't Control Myself," is a perfect example of selective charting. The song was number one in England. In America, it reached the top 40—in *Cashbox* and *Billboard* (which means it was one of the most frequently-played records on pop stations). WMCA chose not to play the song. Station officials simply claim the song never made their chart, which actually means the song was never played because it was never played.

Why? A good guess is that lyrics like these stepped just a little too far over the opaque blue-line:

If you knew me like I know you girl,
Your knees would bend and your hair would curl . . .

However, behind disc jockeys' use of the omnipotent bullets to guide airplay choices lies a neglected fallacy. *Billboard* and *Cashbox* use airplay charts to determine their own standings. This means, in effect, that disc jockeys are depending on each other's taste (not the public's) in programming for the massive pop audience. It means that your musical tastes are formed by a hard core of disc jockeys on confidential "breakout" stations. It means records compete in a market that is anything but open. And it means that the entire process of hit-making is an inside operation into which consumer-preference has only incidental effect.

Thus the success of a truly innovative record is a remarkable event. Every once in a while experimental sound works around the establishment and actually forces its way into the public's consciousness. But the ranks close quickly behind, leaving much of the honest sweating truth of rock 'n' roll on the shelves and presenting a platter of corpses on wax.

The public is only incidentally responsible for bland popular art. The men who keep music sterile are the trendmakers themselves— the ones who play the hits play the hits play the hits.

Inadvertently, they are creating a popular underground. What the journalist must do is to bring this underground to the surface where it can sprout and bear fruit—little red bullets.

—THE VILLAGE VOICE, 1967

# ● GIRAFFE HUNTERS

Shapes of things:

Connie De Nave holds a press conference for the Yardbirds (fresh from frozen England) in the Hotel Americana's Provence Room. See, there's this Provincial gold lamé wallpaper—that's how it got its name.

Amid the Acrilan rugs and the Miami Beach miasma, reporters fire sugary questions at the boys in the Chelsea Antiques Market gear. Jeff Beck tells us how: "Each of us has his own scene inside his head when we play." Chris Dreja reveals: "The Carnaby bit is a drag. People realize that whatever they buy—even if it's fresh from the shop—they'll walk down the street and see everyone wearing it."

Reporters cluster around the liquor cart in back of the room. Connie De Nave herself puts down the immigration authorities for refusing to consider the Yardbirds unique. The lady reporters size the boys up, and the boys respond with winks and Buster Brown grins.

Keith Relf wins most of the votes for his groupie story: "I had fifteen letters from a girl after I told some reporters I liked rhubarb crumble, which is a kind of fruitish pudding. She said she was the best rhubarb-crumble maker going. I had people write her and say I was married; I tried everything, but she kept writing, saying I had to eat her rhubarb crumble."

The methodic sound of scribbling. "What finally happened?"

215

The answer is lost in another question, and the Queen of Rhubarb Crumble is left with recipe in hand. The press conference ends that way—as uneventful, as pre-cooked, as soppy as a warmed-over can of hash.

This week's reality is a lot like that dismal affair. It stares brazenly at you over coffee and danish when the conversation turns to squinting whispers over the affair between an editor and a "heavy" guitarist slated for a major piece that month. Your informer's eyes narrow, she sips her tea between syllables, and explains in perfect lady journalese: "That, my dear, is a hard cock to follow."

Reality rings every weekday morning at 10 A.M., in a parade of coiffed agents and spangled public relations men who sing the praises of clients on one hand and offer gifties—FREE FREE FREE—on seven others. The Swarthmore voice confides: "I just had to tell you before Sue Szekely, dear, but we're holding a private luncheon, dear, for Peter Noone, and I know you'd. . . ."

The real interview: his press agent sits alongside a pile of printed bios—the letterhead bears the greeting: *Gnus for Youse.* The agent grooms and coaxes his budding superstar with combing strokes in his voice. "Tell Dick about the time you slipped Bobby Dylan an exploding cigar . . . you'll really want to use this story Dick, I know you will."

In the real world, little red dots tell you which records to watch. In the real world, the crooner of candy-cane ballads is sleeping with his manservant. In the real world, Dick Clark smiles a sour-cream grin over a pack of bad-breath mints while the Action Kids turn cartwheels over a song about racial discontent masquerading as a cha-cha. The radio station that won't play music advocating taking "toxins" distributes a record magazine with a "psychedelic special." Very real.

Reality in pop music is always lying around waiting to be written up. But this passivity is deceptive, because the real world of teen culture is so heavily soaked in greasepaint that it slips and slides through your fingers, always visible as a disguise but never solid enough to grip and dissect.

God may be dead. Wallace may win. It may finally be proven that a steady exposure to flashing lights and deafening music causes

cancer of the coccyx. No matter—they will keep churning out the Sound. Like the old man says: between the idea and the reality, between the emotion and the act, falls the shadow.

This week's reality is all in the shade.

Who makes a superstar? What makes an art form? Who connects desire with spasm, and meshes need with product? Who tells the kids under the el in Astoria what to sing? Who fills Plato's cave with Martha and the Vandellas? Why are the very kids who ring the registers over supersonic sounds also lapping up Paul Revere and the Raiders? It's like eating Caviar on melba toast, but the kids don't seem to be getting indigestion. The question is— who taught them to eat like that in the first place?

What's next: barrio-rock; blueblood-bluegrass; a chamber orchestra playing Chuck Berry; Kate Smith eating avocados?

When I find out, I'll tell. If I don't, I'll guess anyway.

In college, they showed us an anthropology film about a tribe in Africa in the middle of a ferocious famine, and the men had to go out hunting giraffes, with water slung over their shoulders; singing, walking for arid days, trying to smell giraffe dung in the dust clouds, until finally, over a distant ridge, they saw just the neck of an enormous giraffe with spots like brown eyes. As it smelled them its feet churned and its neck waved panicky in the wind—glorious in color—but the men whooped, shook their singing bolos overhead, and ran after the animal; it leapt, careening, and the men tossed their weapons at the animal's legs—legs spread apart for distance—until, hit once, again, it fell straight on its head like the log of the century, fell over itself, neck bending in rubber knots, feet tangled in goat-guts, fell on its face, waiting, and as the men slashed with their knives, the animal's eyes closed slowly, heavily, lids quivering. When they had sliced it up—they show you this in the film—they ate the testicles for power, and then they filled their gourds with blood and slung the hollow animal on poles over their shoulders, and when they marched back to the village there was a feast for days, and the giraffe's head, still proud and sleek, adorned the chief's hut as a trophy.

Rock 'n' roll is the giraffe. Public relations men, disc jockeys, emcees, executives, socko-boffo copy boys, fabulous blondes, proph-

ets, frauds, fakes, connect-the-dots copies, and under-assistant West Coast promo men hunt with their snares and bolos cut, castrate, slice up the meat, and hang shaggy heads in trophy.

I love the giraffe for its color, its coat, and its bobbing neck. I love to watch it run. So I try not to watch when I see it fall, and I see it fall all the time. People like me are good at loving giraffes, but we can't save them. That's up to you.

—THE VILLAGE VOICE, 1966

# AMERICA, THE BEAUTIFUL

Riding easy from Los Angeles on the Superchief express, the whole country seems to reek of What They Have Done To It. You imagined the desert as a vast inconsolable palm, but here it is before you—a series of vacant lots strewn with stripped Oldsmobiles. You remember Mark Strand's poem about the "blue-eyed government," and it's very much in evidence here. You pass your first Indian settlement—a fact conveniently noted on a sign planted by the railroad. The Indians live in adobes or trailers. They don't even wave.

Five minutes at Albuquerque: long enough to touch the kachina dolls in a trading post. Many flags unfurled here—some upside down. Raton, Colorado: they have written that name on the side of a mountain to prove it's really there. Stern flowers. Fresh paint on old fences. The streets are empty at midafternoon.

Sitting in your swivelchair in the climate-controlled observation car feels like being sealed inside a pneumatic tube. The people around you—good folks from the midlands—are taking pictures of the buttes. They are mostly old men and women, afraid of flying, or simply into the dignity of a breakfast served by colored porters in crisp bow ties. You watch them over the Chicago papers (story about "Good Samaritans in Blue") and they watch back.

Lady with the limp prairie drawl spends most of Arizona talking about her dog who up 'n' died, and her son, who plays in the band at Disneyland. Once—in Kansas, perhaps—we pass a pair of bikers.

219

And this lady draws her lips together, takes dead aim with her eyes, and pulls the shades down around her.

That's how "Easy Rider" begins for me. I don't know how it began for Peter Fonda, its producer and star. But he's had plenty of time to think about the film he's always wanted to make (pan shot of a young actor on the set of some grade-B acid flick, jotting down his dreams on the back cover of a Byrds album). And what if some groover with expense-account chits in all his pockets confronted our man with a formal proposition: "Hey, let's make a Peter Fonda movie. It'll have bikes—big steel mothers, with the heavy-metal-thunder understood. And grass—because no one looks as good-looking stoned as Peter Fonda. And lots of that gentle fingertip sex kids are so famous for (when they're not immersed in rape and pillage). But this time, let's make a Peter Fonda movie that transcends being a Peter Fonda movie. The way 'Bonnie and Clyde' transcended being a film about Bonnie and Clyde.

"Let's make it authentic, down to the mannerisms and slang. Let's make it independent, so we don't have to include a theme song by the Association. And let's make it shine America—the land as harsh and eager as everyone knows it must be somewhere. Beyond what's visible from an observation car. The forgotten America —and all the people in it. People you've never met, but you know they exist because you don't see them on TV.

"Let's make a film about a new hero. Call him Wyatt . . . lofty Old West name. Dress him in soft leather and shades. With a pointy chin. He looks scrawny naked, but you can tell he's good in bed. His big line is: 'Think I'm gonna crash.' He spends whole scenes watching things. And his best friend, Billy, calls him Captain America.

"What d'ya say, Peter?"

And Peter Fonda says yes, because he's always wanted to do a *real* Peter Fonda movie. The kind where the bikers don't plow through wheat fields to take a short cut, and where the dialogue runs like this:

"You ever want to be anyone else?"

"I'd like to try Porky Pig."

"I never wanted to be anyone else."

Ultimately, that's what "Easy Rider" is: the world's first *real* Peter Fonda movie. Nothing heroic, like John Wayne at the Alamo. You can't detect any of that charisma-of-the-silver-screen in Peter Fonda's performance. He's not even trying to resurrect the love-me-I'm-sensitive syndrome of the Fifties. He's just, you know, gettin' his thing together. The cool of acting natchrully; that's why you don't get embarrassed watching him turn on.

But notice how you notice Peter Fonda despite all that panamericana. Despite Dennis Hopper, who directs the film with a heavy but steady hand, and whose performance as Billy is the most vivid evocation of California hip-uptight you'll ever see on screen. Despite even Terry Southern, who gets credit for the screenplay along with Hopper and Fonda, and who must be responsible for the delicate rage this film projects.

Despite all this—it's Peter Fonda's ride. His gangly grace (which must be considered freaky by Vistavision standards) was only a prop in those Roger Corman shockers. But now that he has the parallel cools of actor-writer-producer going for him, it's finally been realized.

That wouldn't matter much, except that Fonda's Captain America also embodies an entire culture—its heroes and its myths. That's what's most real about this film. It dreams well. Like a real revolution, or a real Spiro Agnew speech. And that alone is why it's worth a suspension of disbelief.

Except, myths don't mean much to nonbelievers. And I'm afraid some straight critics aren't going to see beneath the stars and stripes on Captain America's back. To a professional, "Easy Rider" might seem a terribly simplistic job of moviemaking. Naive is the word. Naive enough to pit a groovy, long-haired hero against a vicious crew-cut system, represented by policemen, motel managers, truck drivers, and just-folks. Naive enough to show us noble cowboys, smiling Mexicans and whores with hearts—all the good people dispossessed or alienated from the source of power. Naive enough for jump cuts and overexposed film and hazy fades and lines like: "I'm hip about time."

But, ever think about how close being naive is to being beautiful? Consider how sacred naiveté is in rock. Why, the Beatles would sacrifice 46 of their 48 channels to recapture it. And Dylan had to cut his hair and "throw it all away" to seem naive again. There's something terribly powerful about being simple these days, as though the only true artists are people who don't know any better.

That's why "Easy Rider" comes so close to capturing the feel of rock on film. And that's why the score (which is simply a dozen very good songs) seems so natural. It's almost like hearing music in a car—Jimi Hendrix against a Louisiana landscape; Steppenwolf out on the freeway; the Band wailing across the desert like electric coyotes. But there's that extra dimension because this is a Peter Fonda movie, and they're about to light up and talk about bugs.

The press releases say "Easy Rider" is structured like a ballad, and you can sense that even if you don't know it. Saga of two friends who run some dope in from Mexico, and use the money to bankroll a trip to the Mardi Gras. They travel through the Southwest and their heads change with the scenery. Each verse is an incident, an encounter, or a confrontation. Each chorus is just Wyatt and Billy on the road. And music—especially music.

Andrew Sarris, who knows a lot more about movies than I do (but perhaps less about Captain America), thinks all this is silly. And it is. Silly as a chili dog, or wig city. Silly as rock 'n' roll music. Silly as an astronaut on the moon.

I guess I really need to believe in that kind of silliness. Because the adventures of Captain America seem terribly moving to me. Give me chills, because they suggest that if you separate the land and technology of America from its politics, you have a valid basis for patriotism. It may seem dialectically and esthetically unsound, but I want to believe that "Easy Rider" is a travel poster for the new America.

That's why it makes me angry to remember that Wyatt and his friend never do make it. They are systematically destroyed—busted, beaten, and finally extinguished by the blue-eyed government and its forgotten constituents. I don't mind telling you, that scene's a bit more jolting than the final verse of "Barbara Allen."

What it suggests to me is that naiveté is becoming a luxury around

here. And if you don't believe it, travel East from Los Angeles on the Superchief. And when your car rolls past Cairo, Illinois, take a long look out the window. With the shades rolled up.

Then get silly at your own risk.

—THE NEW YORK TIMES, 1969

# ● INDEX